Wildlife Walkabouts:
Avon and Somerset Border

10 short walks described by
Michael Woods

Illustrated by Julia Morland

To Jane, Thanks for all your hard work and humour during the year. It was great.
Jane x

WAYSIDE BOOKS
CLEVEDON, AVON

Other books in the *Wildlife Walkabouts* series:
    South Cotswolds and North Avon   (ISBN 0-948264-02-0 Pbk)
    Birmingham and the Black Country (ISBN 0-948264-04-7 Pbk)
    The Lizard to Mid-Cornwall   (ISBN 0-948264-03-9 Pbk)

These books are available in most good bookshops, especially in the areas they cover, but in case of any difficulty please contact the publishers:

Wayside Books, 3 Park Road, Clevedon, Avon BS21 7JG
Telephone (0272) 874750

British Library Cataloguing in Publication Data

Wildlife walkabouts. – New ed.
  Avon and Somerset border : 10 short walks.
  1. England. Organisms
  I. Woods, Michael, *1948–*
574.942

ISBN 0-948264-05-5

First edition published in 1985

Second edition published in 1989
Second impression 1992

Text copyright © 1985, 1989 Michael Woods
Illustrations copyright © 1985, 1989 Julia Morland, unless otherwise credited
Photographs copyright © 1989 Paul Glendall, Clevedon, Avon

Design, make-up and maps by Ralph Sandoe, Wayside Books

Wildlife Walkabouts series copy-edited by Edward Sparkes, Clifton, Bristol

Typeset by Wayside Books, Clevedon, Avon BS21 7JG
Reproduction by Westspring Graphics, Weston-super-Mare, Avon BS23 IQF
Printed and bound by Short Run Press Ltd, Exeter, Devon

*To the publisher's children,
Clare and Alexandra, and, naturally,
to the Woods.*

David Pearce recording a programme for BBC Radio Bristol's 'Wild West Show' on the Bourton Combe walk with author Michael Woods, illustrator Julia Morland and 'budding' naturalists Katie Pearce with Clare and Alexandra Sandoe

Acknowledgements

This book would not have been possible without help from the following people: my father, Doug Woods; Chris and Mary Potts; Alec Coles and Jane Evans; John Boyd; Janet Gardner; Julia Morland for her fine illustrations, and Ralph Sandoe who conceived and produced the project — to each and every one of you, thank you.

Publisher's Note

This is the second edition of *Wildlife Walkabouts: Avon and Somerset Border* and is one of five published so far in the series. The publisher anticipates producing others covering different areas. With this in mind the publisher and author welcome any constructive criticism, praise or additional information from readers on any aspect of this publication. Please write to the publisher, or author, at Wayside Books, 3 Park Road, Clevedon, Avon BS21 7JG.

Permission to photocopy. The author and illustrator have given their kind permission for the owner of this book to obtain a single photocopy of any page or pages between 9 and 108 inclusive for personal use whilst walking the routes. If the book itself is used on the walks, a protective plastic cover, obtainable from most good booksellers and stationers, would help to keep it in good condition.

Where the routes of these walks cross private land, they are believed to follow public footpaths which were in existence at the time of going to press. No responsibility can be taken by the author or the publisher for any errors in this book and particularly for any action which may be taken against its readers and users as a result of these.

CONTENTS

List of Illustrations in Text 6
Introduction by Michael Woods 7
Country Code 8

The Walks:
    Bourton Combe 9
    Blagdon and Butcombe 19
    Westhay Moor 29
    Litton 39
    King's Castle, Wells 49
    Black Down 59
    Sand Point 69
    Yatton 79
    Brent Knoll 89
    Berrow 99

Keys to Identifying Wildlife 109
    Birds 110
    Plants 113
    Ferns 114
    Trees 115
    Mammals 116
    Sea Shells 120
    Insects and Spiders 121

Wildlife and the Law 122
List of Organisations 123
Bibliography 124
Index 125
Other Books in the Series 128

LIST OF ILLUSTRATIONS IN TEXT

Adder (viper) 67
Alder, common 32
Ash 61

Badger 15, 55
Barnacle, acorn, Australian and British 76
Barnacle, goose 107
Bilberry see Whortleberry
Bittersweet (woody nightshade) 28
Black bryony 93
Blackthorn 92
Blaeberry see Whortleberry
Bulrush (greater reedmace) 37
Burdock 32

Chickweed 35
Cinnabar moth 104
Coot 47
Cross leaved heath 64
Curlew 106

Dandelion 36
Dog fish, lesser spotted, and egg case (mermaid's purse) 108
Dogwood 53
Dormouse 13
Dunlin 105
Dunnock (hedge-sparrow) 81

Elder 77
Elm bark beetle galleries 46

Fox 41
Frog, common 85

Gatekeeper 57
Goldfinch 83
Grass snake 85
Greater horseshoe bat 66
Greater reedmace see Bulrush
Groundsel 36

Hare 38
Hawkmoth, privet 95
Heather, bell 64
Heather, common (ling) 64

Hedgehog 58
Hedge-sparrow see Dunnock
Hemp agrimony 27
Hermit crab 75
Heron 83
Honeysuckle 95

Ivy 12

Jay 16

Kestrel 84
Kingfisher 33

Lapwing see Peewit
Larch 45
Ling see Heather, common

Magpie 97
Mallard 77
Maple, field 56
Marram grass 103
Mendip profile 63
Mermaid's purse see Ray (common) and Dog fish
Milk churn 96
Moorhen 47

Nightshade, woody see Bittersweet

Oak, English (pedunculate) 11
Oak, Turkey 11
Old man's beard 71
Otter 34
Oyster catcher 106

Peacock 44
Pedunculate oak see Oak, English
Peewit (lapwing) 38
Pipistrelle bat 91
Primrose, evening 103
Privet 92
Purple loosestrife 22

Rabbit guard, tree with 93
Ragwort 104
Ray, common (skate), and egg case (mermaid's purse) 107

Red admiral 44
Red valerian 43
Rock samphire 72
Roe deer 18
Rowan 68
Ruddy darter dragonfly 37

Sanderling 105
Sand Point soil/rock profile 74
Scots pine 35
Scurvy grass 72
Shelduck 107
Shoveler 23
Shrew, common 84
Silage bags 95
Skate see Ray (common)
Small tortoiseshell 43
Southern hawker dragonfly 37
Speckled wood 57
Squirrel, grey, and winter drey 87
Stonechat 65
Swan, mute 88
Sycamore 98

Teasel 36
Thistle 83
Thrift 72
Tit, coal 15
Toad, common 102
Tufted duck 48

Viper see Adder
Vole, field 82

Wagtail, pied 48
Warbler, reed 43
Wheatear 65
White, large cabbage 62
White, marbled 62
White poplar 78
Whortleberry (Bilberry, Blaeberry) 63
Witches' broom 33
Woodmouse 84
Woodpecker, green 17
Woody nightshade see Bittersweet
Wrack, egg, bladder, flat 75
Wren 81

Yew 98

INTRODUCTION

In this book you will find the routes of ten short walks together with a wide range of information about the things you may see when following them. The walks have been deliberately selected to accomplish two things. Firstly, they are all different in terrain, in habitat and, most important, in the variety of wildlife you will come across, and secondly, they avoid, as far as possible, existing nature trails and areas of particular importance for the rare species they contain. If you are lucky enough to come across an unusual orchid or a rare bird, that will be very much your good fortune. I have not led you there for that purpose although I may, perhaps, have opened your eyes to your surroundings on the way.

I have not restricted the walks to any particular season, so a few of the species mentioned may not be around during your visit. On the other hand, you will probably spot some not included in the text that were not to be found when I was there.

In the four years that have passed since I wrote the introduction to the first edition of this book there have been some dramatic environmental changes. While urbanisation and road-building continue apace, there is more encouragement to plant hardwoods rather than softwoods and questions are being raised about agricultural intensification. 'Set Aside' (a scheme that compensates farmers for not growing crops which are in surplus thus potentially allowing land to become more hospitable to wildlife) has been introduced and although acknowledged as not being totally successful, it is at least a step in the right direction. A limited number of Environmentally Sensitive Areas, including the Somerset Levels, have been declared and there is a growing realisation that conservation has a cost. But a cost that is worth meeting. Politicians of every hue are declaring their commitment to 'greenness'.

The countryside is always changing. Let us hope that, in future, these changes will be beneficial rather than detrimental to wildlife and the landscape. Who knows, perhaps the walks in this book will actually improve over time!

Michael Woods
Cheddar, Somerset
1989

COUNTRY CODE

Wherever you go:

Enjoy the countryside and respect its life and work
Guard against all risk of fire
Fasten all gates
Keep dogs under close control
Keep to public paths across farmland
Use gates and stiles to cross fences, hedges and walls
Leave livestock, crops and machinery alone
Take all litter home
Help to keep all water clean
Protect wildlife, plants and trees
Take care on roads especially when crossing
Make no unnecessary noise
Park considerately
Respect local residents

BOURTON COMBE

Bracket fungi thriving on a fallen tree trunk

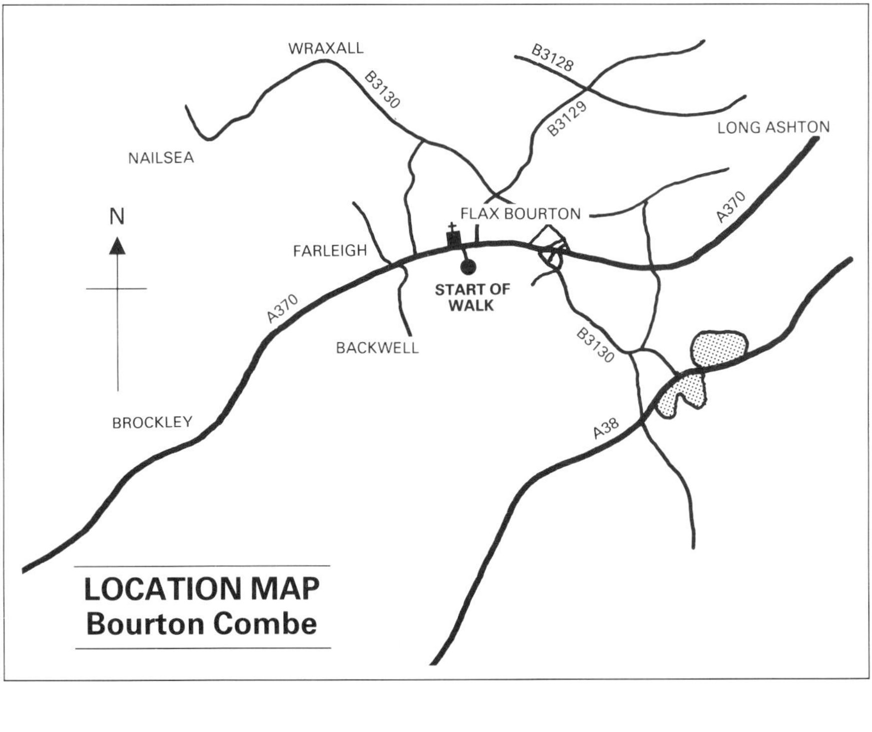

LOCATION MAP
Bourton Combe

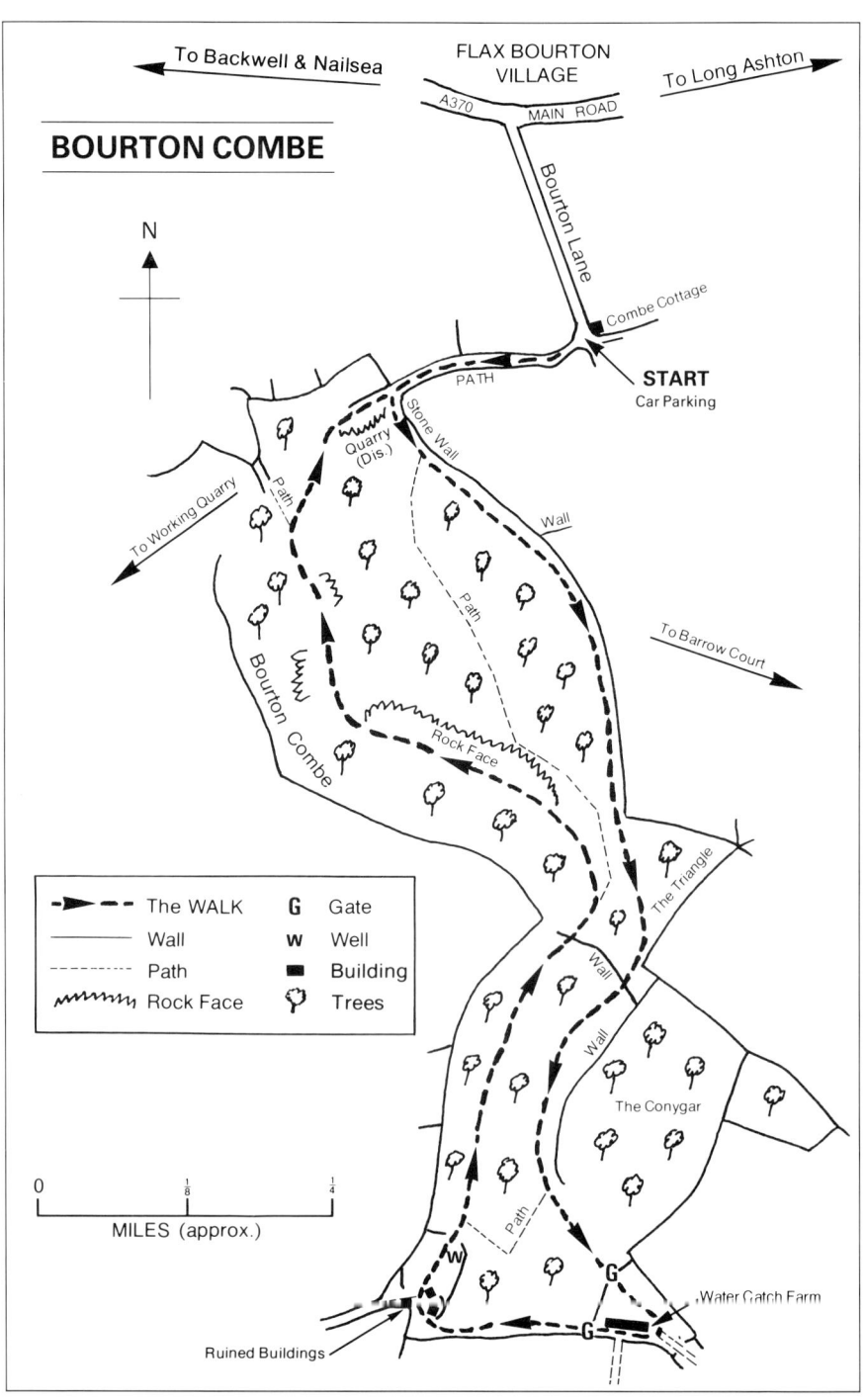

BOURTON COMBE

Grid Ref. OS 182 (1:50 000) 508 690   Approx. 2½ miles

This woodland walk can be damp in places, so wellies are advisable unless it has been fairly dry for some time. Although not flat, there are no steep hills but the rocks underfoot can make the going a bit rough.

If driving, park with consideration at the far end of Bourton Lane near the start of the walk. Take the footpath to the right, signposted 'Barrow Common'.

On this first corner is a group of oak trees which, in autumn, produce acorns in woolly cups. They are Turkey oaks and are of southern European origin. There will be an opportunity to compare them with the so-called English (pedunculate) oak further along the walk. The leaves of the Turkey oak have lobes which are more pointed than those of the native species and the acorn cups of the pedunculate are knobby rather than woolly. Turkey oaks were originally introduced for their rapid growth and have become naturalised in a number of places. If a Turkey oak leaf can be found on the ground here it will be of interest to compare it with those of the pedunculate growing at the end of this track.

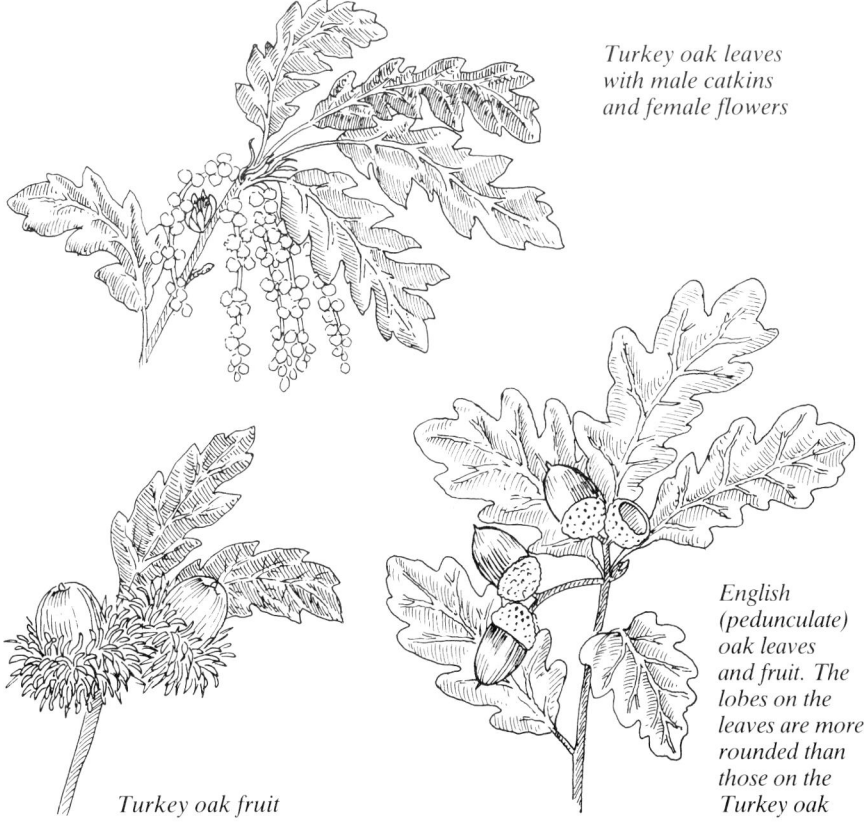

Turkey oak leaves with male catkins and female flowers

English (pedunculate) oak leaves and fruit. The lobes on the leaves are more rounded than those on the Turkey oak

Turkey oak fruit

11

The path here lies at the bottom of a north-facing slope and is very shaded from the sun, this causes it to be damp and therefore a good place for ferns to grow. The most noticeable species here is hart's tongue fern with its long dark-green shiny fronds. These are especially beautiful when fresh and bright in spring as they gradually uncoil. Their name presumably originates from their resemblance to the tongue of a hart or deer.

Also along here soft shield ferns should be encountered. This species is more typically fern-like in appearance and can be identified by its 'thumbs'. One of the two leaflets next to the stalk of the frond is larger than the other and sticks out like a thumb. A closer look will reveal a small 'thumb' at the base of each leaflet as well. On the underside of the leaflets, rows of spores may be seen which are eventually scattered from the plant to produce new ferns. (See illustrations of ferns on page 114.)

There is a good opportunity here to look carefully at ivy leaves. Most people recognise ivy as having shiny dark-green five-lobed leaves and these are especially noticeable on strands of this climbing plant as they snake across the woodland floor seeking a tree to climb. Having found a suitable vertical surface, the plant attaches itself with a special glue and climbs upwards. It uses trees only for support and is not a parasite in any way. Once it reaches a site that has good light, sometimes 50 feet above the ground, its leaves become more oval and pointed, and at this stage it produces flowers. Unlike most other plants, the ivy waits until autumn to flower and thus encourages the attentions of many late flying insects for whom the choice of nectar-bearing flowers is now very limited. It has a very heady scent, slightly reminiscent of the musky smell of otters.

Ivy berries do not ripen fully until early spring when their black bunches are much beloved by birds – who are, by now, very short of food. Although it lives in an apparently hostile environment – closely shaded by forest trees – by reversing the seasons, ivy has made itself needed because of a lack of alternatives, and is also more visible because trees have lost their leaves.

Ivy leaves and flowers.
The flowers do not come out until autumn

Pass through the gap in the stone wall with a gatepost on the left.

On the right here is a fine specimen of a pedunculate oak. It is an easily-recognisable tree, having distinctive leaves and acorns. Even in the middle of winter when these have been shed, this oak can be indentified by its very angular shape with lots of 'elbows' to its branches. There are two common native oaks, the pedunculate and the sessile. On the former the acorns are on long stalks (peduncles) while on the latter the acorn cups are stalkless and bunch together as a result.

Turn left here and walk up the path between the field and the wood.

The first area of woodland consists of old coppiced hazel – hazel bushes which have been continually cut down at about seven-year intervals and then allowed to grow new stems from the stump or 'stool'. The crop of straight stems was once of enormous economic importance in the countryside. They were employed for everything from pea and bean sticks to making hurdles and were also extensively used for making charcoal, not because our forebears had many barbecues, but used for any process requiring extreme heat such as steel-making. Nowadays almost all of these needs are fulfilled in other, more modern, ways and hazel coppicing is a dying skill.

Dormouse

From the point of view of conservation this is most unfortunate as not only does hazel coppice tend to have a particularly rich array of flowers, but it is also the major habitat of the dormouse which is found in this area. This gingery furry-tailed little animal is not very common, emerging only at night to feed on vegetable food. Unfortunately, the demise of the hazel coppice could mean an increasing scarcity of dormice which would be very sad as they are delightful animals.

One can play nature detective and see what small mammals are in this wood by inspecting discarded hazel nuts. If a shell is found with a hole neatly chiselled out of one side and the kernel missing, the feeder could be one of three animals: the woodmouse, the bank vole or, more unusually, the dormouse.

Look carefully at the rim of the hole as marks on both the edge of the hole and on the shell surface are indications of woodmice at work. The bank vole makes no marks on the shell surface but smooths out the inside edge. Search for hazel nut shells along the edge of the path and, using a magnifying glass if necessary, check the rim of the hole. (See illustrations on page 117.)

The catkins of hazel are present throughout winter in a tight retraced form. Early in spring they elongate to form proper 'lambs' tails' and, at this time of the year, tiny red female flowers can be found which will be pollinated by the yellow pollen shed by the male catkins.

The plants in deciduous woodland have evolved to bloom early from bulbs or rhizomes. This foodstore gives them a boost in spring to push out flowers and leaves before the foliage grows on the trees overhead and deprives them of light – bluebells are a good example of this. Here, dog's mercury may be seen –

a plant with a spike of green flowers – and possibly primroses, wood anemones with their delicate white flowers, and ramsons (wild garlic) which have extremely pungent foliage.

In spite of their evolutionary efforts, these flowers are unlikely to grow under the large beech tree (along the path on the right) as the foliage of this tree is generally so dense as to shade out completely plants trying to grow beneath. The tree can be identified in winter by the smooth grey bark on its branches and its brown cigar-shaped buds. Spring time sees delicate downy light-green leaves which gradually darken during summer and then turn golden brown in autumn. The beech seed (mast) consists of triangular nuts held in a case covered with soft spines. The mast is much loved by squirrels and woodmice as well as numerous birds. There are sycamore trees here too, and in summer it is interesting to check their five-lobed leaves for black spots. These are called 'tar spots' and are caused by a fungus.

> *Squirrels can damage sycamore trees by stripping their bark – often leaving it in tatters hanging down the tree. If the bark is removed all round the trunk the tree will die.*

There are many signs of badgers in this wood. Feeding signs may be seen, such as small excavations left after digging for worms, logs overturned or moss scratched up in search of beetles, roots dug up or even large holes left after a wasps' nest has been exhumed and eaten. In this case, the badger, which loves wasp grubs, does not follow the entrance hole into the nest because of the risk of receiving a sting on the nose. Instead, it digs straight down to the nest and relies on its thick coat to deter angry wasps. On the following day, all that remains is a large hole with a few pieces of papery nest and a number of disgruntled adult wasps buzzing around in the bottom.

Badger paths are very evident, trails of hard earth pounded over the centuries by generations of badgers. Where they lead under barbed-wire fences, badger hairs (white at each end and black in the middle) are often left clinging to the barbs and are worth watching out for. (See illustration on page 116.) Being fiercely territorial, their paths have great significance and lead from the main sett to outlying holes, to favourite feeding grounds or watering places, or perhaps around the perimeter itself. Not unnaturally, the animals resent any interruptions to their paths and when man builds a road across an existing path, they continue to follow their route even if the surface itself has changed completely. Nowadays, to avoid accidents, artificial badger tunnels have been built under many new roads.

It is quite possible that a mark across the path may be found with a scattering of grass and leaves on either side as if a dead body had been dragged into the wood – this is a badger bedding trail. Badgers, being comfort-loving animals, like to tuck themselves up underground in a mass of grass and leaves. This bedding has to be renewed from time to time and they will then wander off to find suitable material to collect which they drag backwards to the sett by gripping it under their chin whilst holding it in place with their front paws. As one would expect, quite a lot of the carefully gathered vegetation spills out on the way or is snagged on roots or bushes and this is what will be seen. It is easy to imagine the grunting and shuffling sounds that accompanied these labours of the night.

The path levels out and at this point two tall lime trees can be found. The trees here show many of the typical features of limes: they are the tallest broad-

Badgers

The biggest threat to badgers is man and many are killed on the road

leaved tree in most areas and these two are certainly large specimens. Around their base are dense masses of sprouting twigs and high in the branches are clumps of mistletoe.

The leaves of the lime are heart shaped and in summer can be shiny with honeydew from aphids. As anyone who has parked a car under a lime tree will know, this honeydew falls on everything beneath the tree and the spots turn black with sooty-mould. The leaves sometimes have nail galls attached to them which can be identified by their similarity to red dunces' caps.

The mistletoe seen in winter when the lime is bereft of leaves is a semi-parasitic plant. Its sticky white berries are rubbed into crevices in bark by birds trying to clean their bills. From here the plant sprouts, its branches divide, and divide again, to form the mistletoe bush – if that is what it can be called – so familiar to us all. The plant is either male or female and their flowers, which appear in spring, are wind-pollinated and the berries ripen in time for Christmas, when a sprig may be hung up for kissing beneath. This custom possibly came from ancient fertility rites or perhaps denoted peace and hospitality.

Soon after passing the limes, a very large section of tree trunk on the right will be seen with a good crop of colourful bracket fungi of various species. At this point the wood extends out to the left into an area called The Triangle. Continue along the path through the remains of a wall into a mixture of trees which includes Scots pine and larch on the left. In the tops of these the high notes of tits will sometimes be heard. Great and blue tits, which come to garden bird-tables, will be present in mixed flocks together with coal tits. The latter are slightly smaller than blue

Coal tit

These delightful little birds sometimes visit bird-tables

tits and have white cheeks and a white nape on a black head. They have quite long fine bills with which they probe bark and cones for insects. Sometimes tiny goldcrests will join these tit flocks. Although these birds may not be seen immediately, they should be spotted flitting from one tree to another if the watcher stands still and keeps quiet.

Go through the gate and keep to the left of the farm buildings until the last one is reached. Here, turn sharp right and, with the fields on the left, walk back past the other side of buildings and pass through the gate back into the woods.

There will be a number of large beech trees on the right before reaching two groups of ruined buildings. At the second group, opposite the old barn with stone steps, turn right into the combe again.

Pause here to look at the Scots pine and the larch between the buildings. The larch is a particularly gnarled specimen and, without its needles, has the appearance of an old man with his back bent against the wind. An old well and pump can be seen by the path here which presumably served the steading that once thrived at this point.

The vegetation in this early part of the combe is quite young and airy with spindly sycamore and ash trees reaching up for the light. Rhododendrons start to appear on the left, and although beautiful when in flower, these imports

The brightly-coloured jay with its loud cackling call likes oak woods as it is very partial to acorns. In autumn it buries many as store against severe weather conditions and those remaining undiscovered often take root as new oaks

Green woodpeckers may be seen feeding on ants on the ground

from the Far East are disliked by naturalists because they quickly crowd out native species and can take over a wood completely.

Throughout the wood are hollow trees in various stages of decay and signs of woodpeckers are frequent. These birds are not known for being either quiet or drab. The great spotted woodpecker is a black and white bird with both sexes having a bright-red patch of feathers beneath their tail, and in the male, on the nape of the neck too. While the green woodpecker has similar crimson plumage, this time on its crown, its overall coloration is green-yellow. The great spotted woodpecker communicates by drumming on tree trunks, often choosing hollow trees which resonate better. The green woodpecker, on the other hand, drums rather less and is better known for its laughing cry which has earned it the nickname of 'yaffle'.

> Woodpeckers have feet with two toes pointing forwards and two back so that they can grip more firmly to wood. Their tail feathers are stiff and act as a rigid third point of contact to enable the bird to have a solid base from which to chisel away at the timber.

Woodpeckers eat insects, chipping bark away to reach the invertebrates lurking beneath. Where it is impossible to reach their prey in this way the woodpecker will probe under bark with its long barbed tongue to secure its meal. They also feed on the ground and, if walking quietly, a green woodpecker may be encountered hunting at an ant-hill when it will fly off with its characteristic swooping flight and a cry of alarm.

The path forks here. Keep left on the down-hill arm.

Almost at once on the right is a large old pedunculate oak, the grandfather of the wood, with its boughs showing the typical angular 'elbows' and growing festoons of polypody ferns like something from a tropical rain-forest. This fern prefers dark shady north-facing woodland where there is plenty of moisture. It suffers very badly in hot summers when even the mossy branches of trees, such as this one has, dry up. (See illustration on page 114.)

This is the most exciting part of the wood. Bright and picturesque on snowy days, and cool and shady in high summer. The main tree species here is the yew and these are some of the finest I know – beautiful trees and extremely old, whose bark turns a reddish-orange colour when wet. Often planted in churchyards, the yew has a significant place in the Christian religion and is a symbol of life force. The tree itself is a good nesting site for many bird species and its berries are eaten by mammals as well as birds.

The ground is often damp here because of the shadiness of this deep combe and there will be many tracks in the soft earth. In particular, look out for the delicate cloven-hoofed footprints of the little roe deer that passes through this woodland from time to time. (See illustration on page 119.) It is russet-coloured and a little bigger than a red setter.

Follow the path round to the right and uphill at the fork. Pass the disused quarry on the right and the pedunculate oak seen on the outward journey will be reached. Continue straight on to the metalled lane.

Roe deer

These dainty animals are rarely seen in groups of more than three

BLAGDON and BUTCOMBE

Blagdon Lake has seven miles of bankside

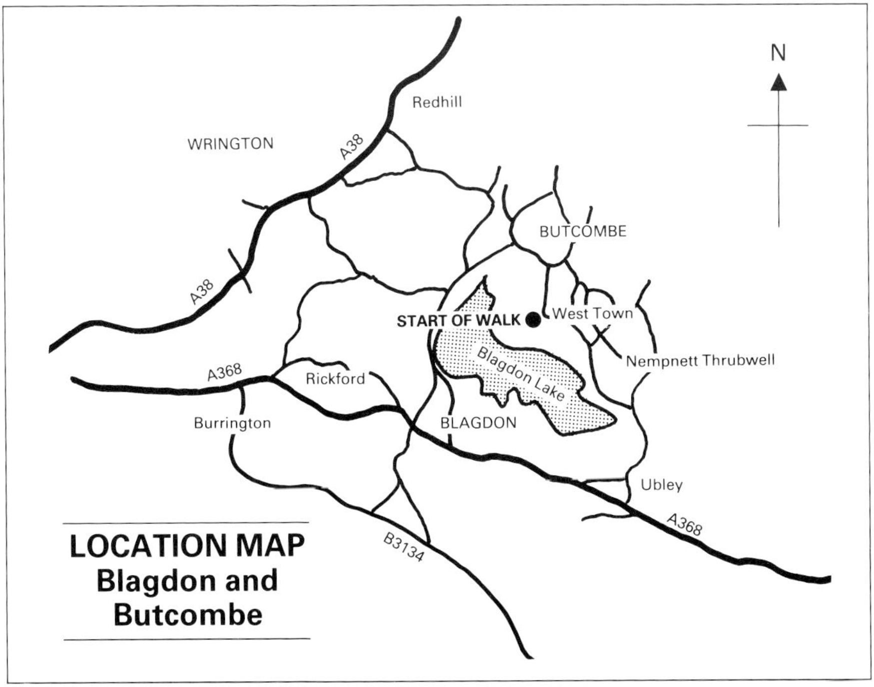

**LOCATION MAP
Blagdon and Butcombe**

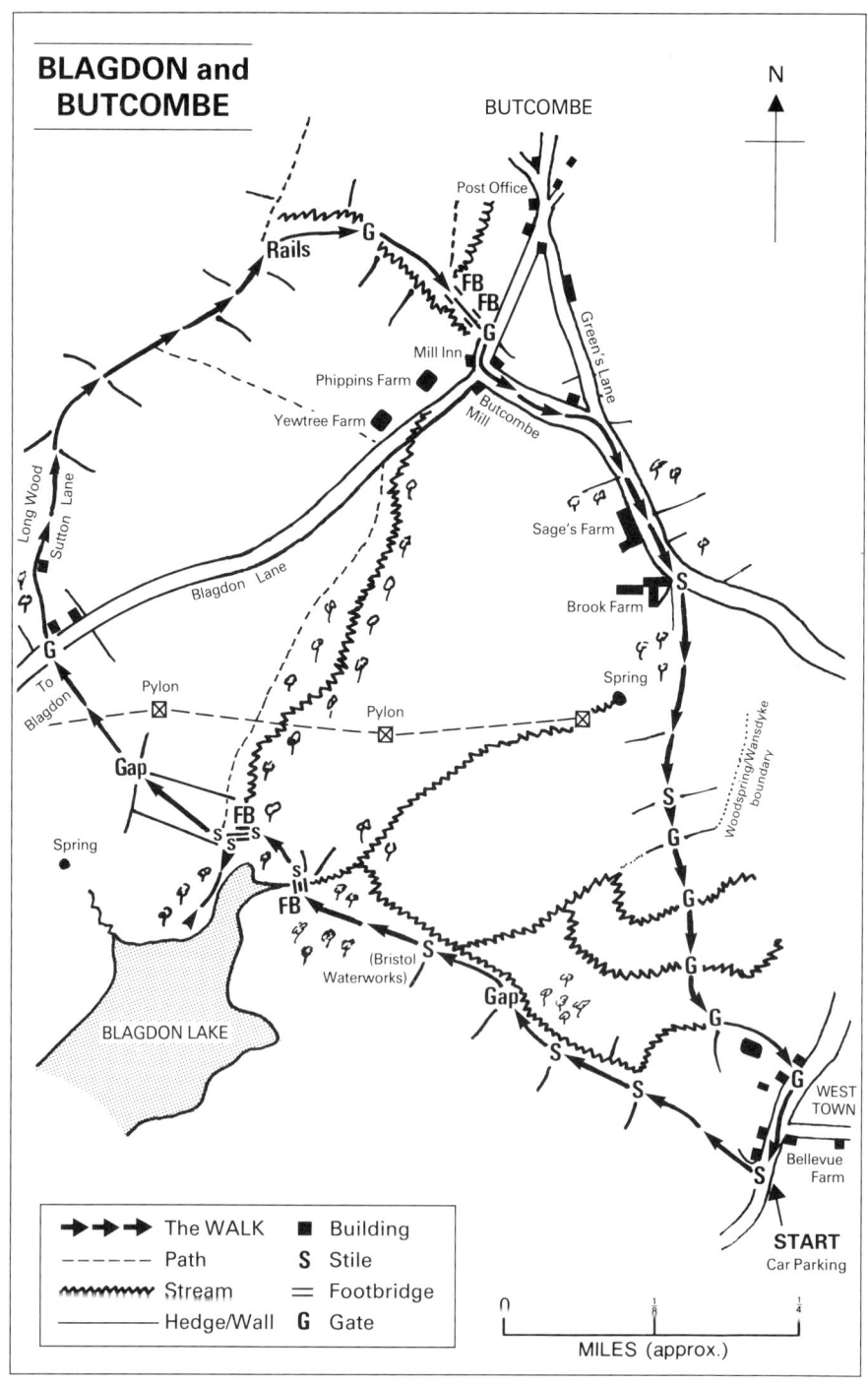

BLAGDON and BUTCOMBE

Grid Ref. OS 182 (1:50 000) 517 604   Approx. 2¼ miles

The walk begins by Blagdon Lake before climbing onto the hills overlooking the lake itself with views across to the highest point on Mendip. There is only one fairly steep uphill section which can be muddy and rough underfoot if the weather has been wet or the local equestrians have been active. The only walk in the book that passes a pub!

Park carefully in the 'No Through Road' which is also marked 'No Access to the Lake' and walk down the lane to the footpath sign on the right. Climb the stone stile and closely follow the wall on the right to its end. From here the cross bars of a stile on the far side of the field can be seen.

There are good views across the lake to Blagdon Village and Coombe Lodge, the large house among the trees. The latter was built by the Wills family and was one of the last large country houses to be erected in England.

Climb the cross-barred stile and follow the hedge on the right.

This is one of a number of rich hedgerows that will be encountered on this walk. Linking the row of large pedunculate oak trees, it contains a wide variety of species including hawthorn and blackthorn, hazel, dogwood, field maple, holly and wild rose. A hedge like this provides a habitat for many birds and animals as well as a superb supply of food and a safe highway from one area to another.

Cross the fallen wooden stile in the corner of the field and walk along the right-hand hedge, passing through the gap into the next field.

Hedgerows are very similar to woodland edges, and for butterflies which live in a woodland edge habitat, such as the speckled wood, whether or not there is a wood behind is often immaterial.

Climb over the stile into Bristol Waterworks Company property.

This piece of woodland is known as All Saints and is managed in accordance with forestry advice provided by Avon Wildlife Trust. The purpose behind the work is to reduce the number of conifers and to increase the varieties of broadleaved trees in order to encourage a greater diversity of animals and birds. On the right-hand side of the path are Corsican pine, larch and Norway spruce, most of which have remained untouched in the new scheme. Look for mixed flocks of tits flitting through the tree-tops here.

> *Norway spruce, as its name suggests, is an introduced species. Although best known as the Christmas tree, its white wood, called deal, is widely used in house interiors and turpentine is extracted from its trunk.*

On the left a large number of trees have been felled and only a few remain to reduce the impact of the reafforestation programme. The planting on this side consists of oak, ash, wild cherry, white beam and lime, although ash is the most obvious species. Many tall plants grow among the trees at this point, especially angelica, rosebay willowherb and creeping thistle. The whole area will be favoured by foxes who make good use of such thick cover to lie-up during the day. Look out for damsel flies all along this path on summer days, which will probably be hunting for insect prey or maybe seeking a mate.

Cross the bridge which spans one of the reservoir's feeder streams and then the stile. Keeping to the left-hand hedge, make for the stile in the corner of the field which guards another footbridge.

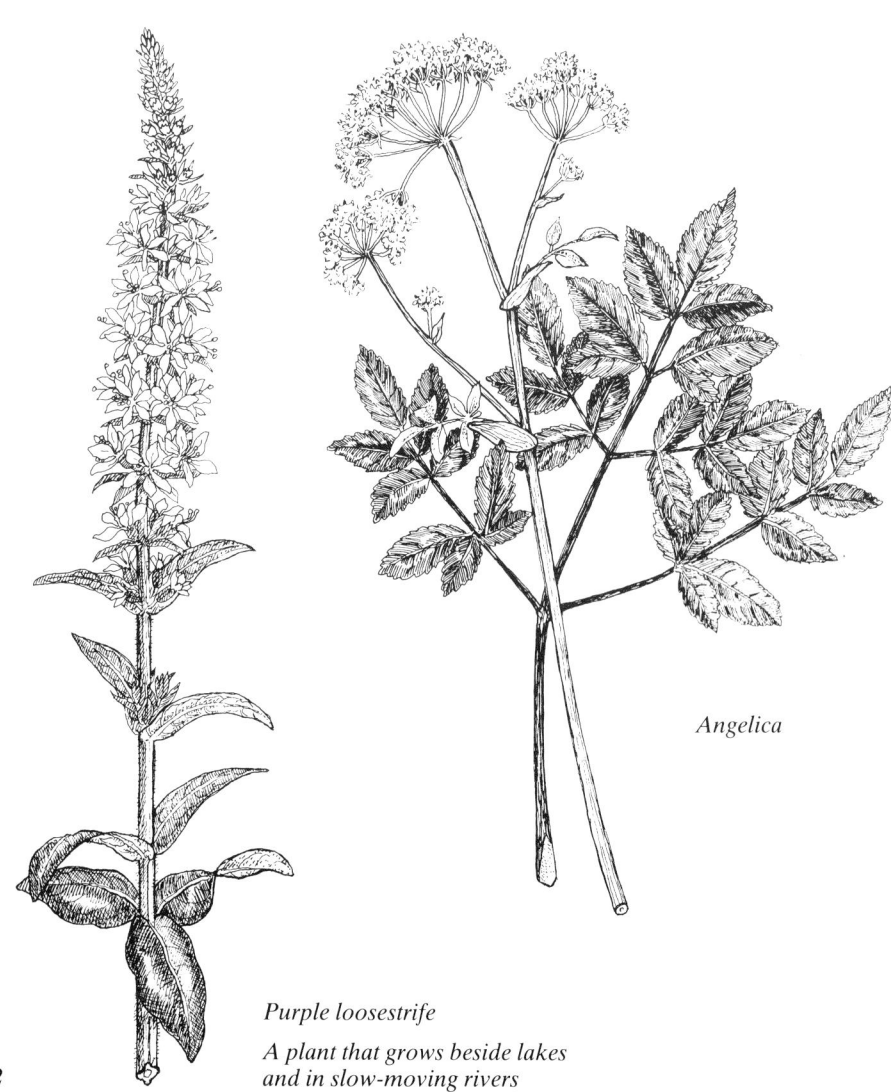

Angelica

Purple loosestrife
A plant that grows beside lakes and in slow-moving rivers

The beautiful spikes of purple loosestrife may be seen here in summer for it is a plant that grows beside lakes and in slow-moving rivers, while another pink-purple flower which enjoys a similar habitat – hairy willowherb – is also present.

Once over the bridge, a short diversion to Blagdon Lake may be taken by climbing the stile on the left and following the path to the lake.

Just how much of a rise and fall there is in the levels can be judged by the marks on the tree trunks when the water is low. Blagdon Lake is said to have a capacity of about 1,700 million gallons and covers an area of 550 acres. It was built at the turn of the century and is reputed to be the first water-supply reservoir to be opened for public fishing. It is now designated a Site of Special Scientific Interest (SSSI) and has an abundance of waterfowl. By using the waterside trees as cover good views of the birds on the water can be obtained. Herons, in particular, like to fish along the shores of this inlet and quite a number may be counted if approached with enough caution.

Several several species of duck should be spotted here, especially in winter when they gather in flocks. Mallard are seen commonly and, because of its great beauty, the plumage of the male is worth studying through binoculars given the opportunity.

Shovelers also congregate in this area and, like the mallard drake, the male has a bottle-green head. The plumage resemblance largely ends with this, for the shoveler has a dark back and chestnut belly while its breast and the area of its lower abdomen are white. Even from a distance it is an easy duck to identify for the white patches fore and aft are very striking and often recognition is aided by its characteristic dabbling behaviour. They are more specialised surface feeders than mallards and rarely upend to bottom feed like the latter. Instead the shoveler holds its head low, with its large bill extended before it, and swims rapidly about using its tongue to pump water in and out of its beak. A fine comb of projections along the edges of its bill ensure that small food items, drawn in with the water, are secured.

Shoveler ducks

Male *Female*

The bill of the shoveler is specially suited for surface feeding

Great crested grebe may also be seen here. In its striking summer plumage, with its frill and black 'ears', it is an easy species to spot especially if it is indulging in its well-known display behaviour. In winter this bird takes on a colder grey and white coloration and is often hard to pick out against the choppy slate waters of the reservoir, particularly when diving frequently to feed. The biggest clue to its identity will be the noticeable flat top to its head.

If the diversion was taken, return to the bridge via the stile and climb another stile a few yards further on into the field. Take a diagonal line towards the top right-hand corner.

In the hedge on the right are a number of Turkey oaks, recognisable by the more pointed lobes on their leaves and by their acorn cups which are covered with soft spines.

Pass through the gap in the field boundary and follow the left-hand hedge to the metal gate by the lane.

In this location during July and August copper-coloured butterflies called small skippers may be seen. These have a different appearance from most butterflies for at rest they may hold their forewings in a slightly raised position with their hindwings angled back like a swing-wing aircraft. They feed on the nectar of a multitude of wild flowers including dandelions, thistles, knapweeds and mayweeds. Their eggs are laid in groups along the inside of the curled edges of soft grasses such as Timothy or Yorkshire fog. Soon after hatching, the young caterpillars hibernate for the winter in a small cocoon of silk. Those that survive come out in spring to munch away at the fresh grasses until it is time to pupate before emerging as a new generation of skippers.

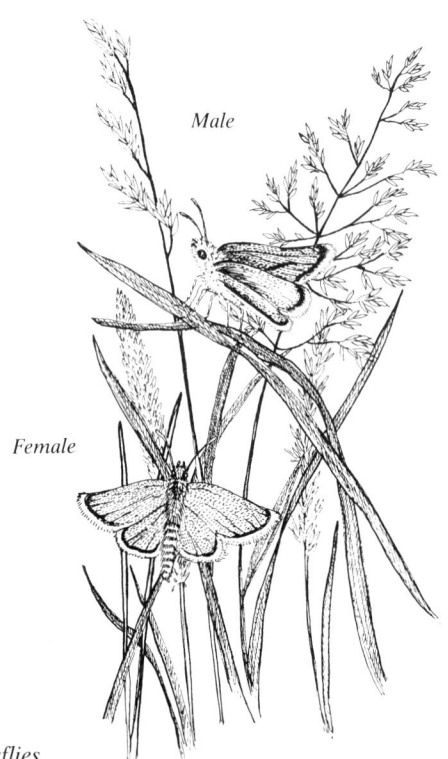

Male

Female

The skipper butterfly is so-called because of its habit of skipping from plant to plant and chasing away other insects. It is more manoeuverable than other butterflies because its wings are proportionately smaller. It could never be said to 'flutter by'.

Small skipper butterflies

Blue butterflies may also be seen here. These are most likely to be the common blue. The male has metallic-blue wings which appear to glint in the sun while those of the female are frequently brown with orange markings around the edges. The underwings of both are duller and speckled and provide good camouflage when their wings are held together over their bodies.

Cross Blagdon Lane and walk up the track opposite which is known as Sutton Lane.

Growing at the bottom of the hedgerow shrubs are dog's mercury and enchanter's nightshade both of which are traditional woodland plants which suggests the fields on this side of the lane were once wooded. Dog's mercury is a member of the spurge family. It is a poisonous plant with green petal-less flowers showing early in the spring. It frequently carpets the floors of woodlands with green throughout the summer. Enchanter's nightshade produces its tiny white flowers much later in the year, from June until September, and thereafter bears fruit covered with hooked bristles. It may be recognised at other times by its pointed, almost heart-shaped, leaves. In spite of the ominous-sounding name, it is not a nightshade at all, but a willowherb.

There are frequently members of the crow family to be seen as the hill is climbed. Flocks of jackdaws may mingle with rooks to feed in the fields on either side or sit in the trees close to the path. Jackdaws are smaller than rooks with white eyes and a grey nape to their necks. They are extremely acrobatic fliers and are notorious both for their love of bright objects and for the habit of nesting in chimneypots. By dropping sticks down the chimney until one jams and then piling further sticks on top they are able to produce a firm base on which to construct a nest. In wilder situations they nest in holes in trees or on cliffs; Cheddar Gorge and some of the Mendip quarries have good populations in spring and summer.

The rook is one of the earliest nesting birds. It lives in a large colony called a rookery and revisits its old nest in autumn ready to begin repairs in the new year. One of the largest rookeries recorded is near Aberdeen with more than 6,000 nests.

There are two large fine beech trees alongside the path, one of which is growing around and enveloping an old fence-post. From here there are good views of the surrounding countryside. Below is Blagdon Lake with its seven miles of bankside while, on the horizon, Black Down (see pages 59–68) – the highest point on Mendip – can be seen, together with the plantation known as Rowberrow Warren.

Just before the track bends to the left and trees arch over the pathway, climb over the two metal-covered wooden rails in the hedgerow on the right and make for the left-hand hedge a few yards away. Walk down the steep hill beside this hedge and the deep ditch (Ham's Gully) which runs parallel with it until the gate in the corner of the field is reached.

A number of meadow flowers can be found among the grass of this pasture. Look out for yellow buttercups and ribwort plantain whose large ribbed leaves press down the vegetation around the plant in order to create a space for itself. In the hedgerows the purple flowers of knapweed may be seen if walking in the summer months.

> *The flowers of ribwort plantain were once used in a children's game, a sort of conker match. The flowerheads were beaten against each other until one broke and the other was declared the winner. Apparently they were known as 'soldiers' or 'fighting cocks' as a result.*

Pass through the gate in the left-hand corner and continue on keeping the hedge to the right.

Keep an eye open for the feeding signs of badgers who will find plenty to eat in these damp meadows.

At the bottom of the field is an old footbridge spanning the stream. Make the crossing with great care, for when I was here last the handrail was very rickety and there was a low wire on the far side waiting to trip me!

There are some old waterworks here which used to serve Butcombe Mill. At one time the countryside would have been littered with such minor engineering works to control the flow of water and harness its power for such things as grinding corn. Unfortunately most of them have fallen into disuse. The wooden paddles have long since rotted, the metal cogs have rusted solid and the old mill ponds have silted up or been filled in.

A few yards further proceed over the small stone footbridge. Cross the two-wire fence at a suitable point and make for the gate to the lane.
   Turn right down the hill – keeping to the right-hand side of the road to face oncoming traffic – to The Mill Inn.

If the weather is hot, this may be just the excuse needed to satisfy one's thirst. On the other hand, it may be cold or wet or even both, in which case this hostelry will provide warmth and good cheer! There is a handy brook opposite in which muddy footwear can be cleaned if need be.

Climb the country lane opposite the inn as far as the 'T' junction and turn right into Green's Lane.
   Continue up this cool shady lane between limestone walls passing Sage's Farm. Further on, at the far side of the concrete road leading off to the right into Brook Farm, there is a four-rail wooden stile in the corner of the field. Climb over this and walk alongside the hedge on the right.

Pineapple weed is common here, as it is in many farm gateways, for it is a plant that likes trampled ground. It is strongly scented although the smell does not remind me of pineapples. Instead it brings to mind the hot sunny days of childhood when loads of hay or straw were brought out of the fields on rocking trailers whose wheels crushed this plant in the gateways to send up its scent in clouds. It is an 'introduced' flower having been brought to Britain during the last century. Authorities differ as to its country of origin, some citing north-east Asia and others the United States.

At the far side of the field climb the stile and cross the ditch with care as it can be difficult.

The dampness of the immediate area has created a suitable habitat for hemp agrimony, a tall plant with a reddish stem. It has pinky-white flowers in dense clusters which should be visible between July and September. It is said to get its name from the resemblance of its leaves to those of hemp.

Hemp agrimony

This plant likes damp areas and flowers in the summer months

Walk across the field to the gate where the boundary between the Districts of Woodspring and Wansdyke is crossed. Make for the next gate.

Crossing the fields, look to the right. On a clear day, Weston-super-Mare and the wooded slopes of Worlebury Hill should be readily visible some 12 miles away. The hump of Steep Holm far out in the Bristol Channel and some 17 miles distant may also be seen. Further round to the right, Sutton Lane can be seen running up the hill, tracing the course of the earlier endeavours of this walk.

In autumn and winter peewits (lapwings) use the low-lying fields for feeding and will take off in loose-winged flapping flocks when approached. Listen out too for the rattling chuckle of the green woodpecker for they also seem to like this area.

After passing through this gate and then another, follow the hedge around to yet another gate. Once through pass the gable-end of a cottage and an outhouse. Keep the fence to the left, walk up the track beside the corrugated garage to the gate which leads into the road. Turn right down the hill.

Bittersweet (woody nightshade) clambers over the hedgerow here. Between May and September it produces bright-purple flowers with yellow centres, followed by egg-shaped berries which start out green and pass through yellow to become bright red. Although a member of the nightshade family and very poisonous, it is often erroneously called deadly nightshade.

Continue down the hill to return to where the walk started.

Bittersweet (woody nightshade)

WESTHAY MOOR

The long straight rows of peat diggings

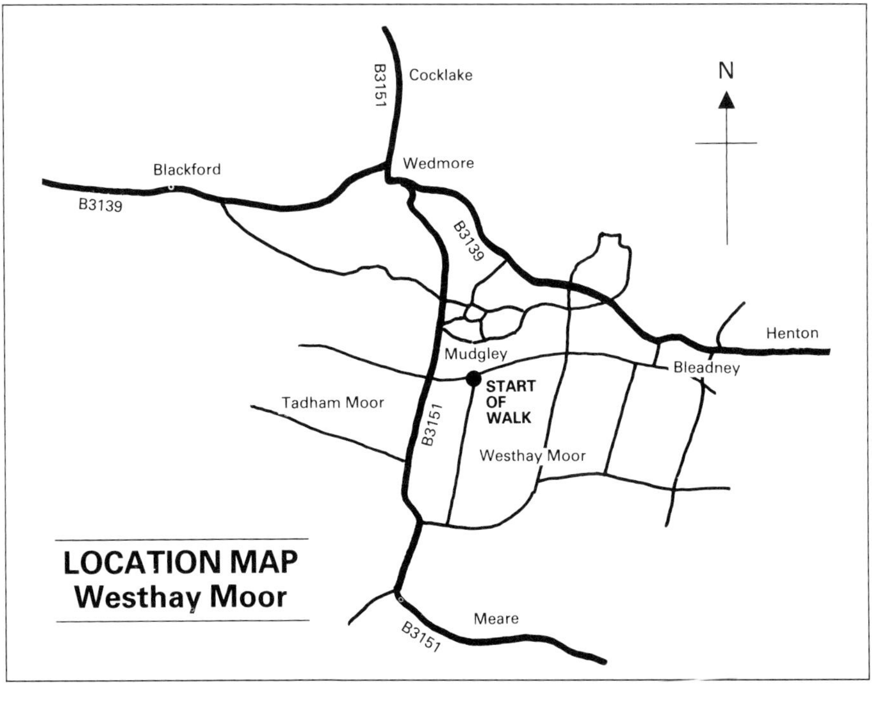

LOCATION MAP
Westhay Moor

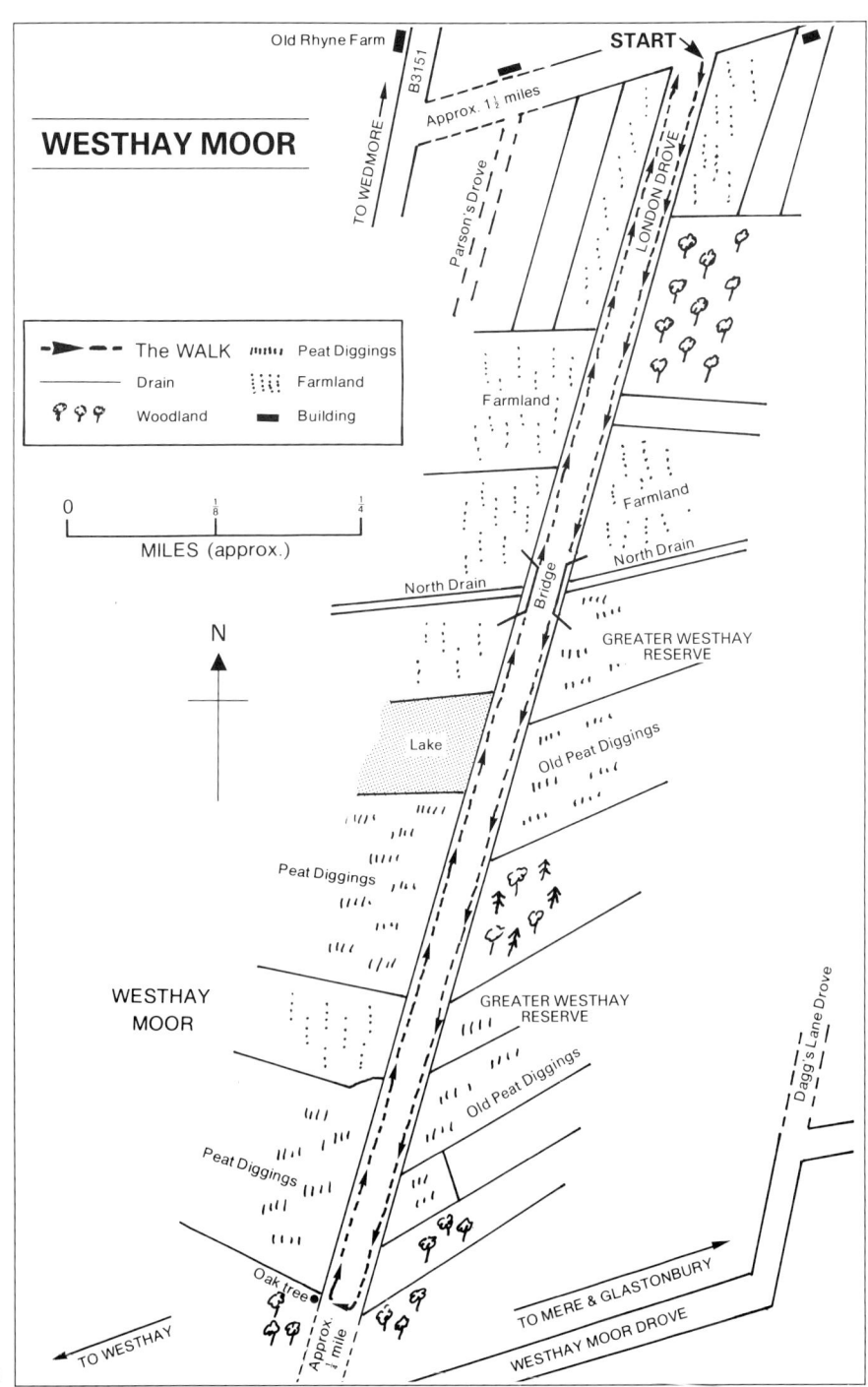

WESTHAY MOOR

Grid Ref. OS 182 (1:50 000) 454 453　　　　　　　　　　　Approx. 2 miles
A flat walk along a drove passing through a nature reserve which includes a lake.

Anyone living on the hills surrounding the levels and moors will know how frequently this area is shrouded in mist; a thin layer of white cloud with the dark skeletal forms of trees protruding through it. To venture into that mist is an eerie experience. It is a silent clammy world where stock move as quiet ghostly figures; grey shapes on a grey ground, looming in and out of sight. Pigeons may crash out of trees when approached or perhaps a heron with a loud 'fraank' will take to laborious flight as a walker appears suddenly out of the fog, getting far closer than the heron would normally permit. A watery sun – a bright white circle in a white sky – pierces through the moving vapour, gradually lifting and thinning the mist until it finally departs completely.

Maybe it is winter when the bare-banked rhynes may be thick with ice which, when broken, reveals deep-brown water remarkably clear for all its peat-staining. Hoar-frost clings to everything; ice jewels glisten on the fine boney stems which formerly bore the long-departed white flowers of cow parsley. A gate-post is thickened by a coating of frost and a nearby plank bridge bears the black prints of a fox where warm pads have melted the ice.

Spring brings winds hurtling in from the Atlantic with nothing to impede their passage. Willow trees bend and lash, the river is lifted into waves and white foam collects among the reeds. Rooks and crows take to the wing from the fields and are immediately carried away, while smaller birds cower in the cover of thickets. Rain, and sometimes hail, arrives in sheets bearing down in slanting curtains and stinging hands and face.

A summer walk is a different tale: high above, larks sing noisily or parachute down on half-closed wings. The heavy scent of meadowsweet hangs on the balmy air and yellow irises colour the banks of the rhynes now green and thick with vegetation. Peewits tumble and cry, their crests akimbo and swans swim idly past accompanied by fluffy cygnets.

Park at the end of the track being careful not to block any entrance. I have concentrated on the left of the path throughout as the walk returns along the same route.

The first large tree on the far side of the ditch (rhyne) is an alder and is typical of wet ground. Nitrogen is essential to plant growth and in boggy areas, where the soil is waterlogged, this element is scarce. Alder roots form an association with a bacteria which enables them to extract nitrogen from the atmosphere thus permitting it to grow in places where other trees cannot. Furthermore, the tree actually puts nitrogen into the surrounding soil. This increased fertility, together with the gradual raising of the ground-level by shed alder leaves, dead branches and, finally, by the trees themselves falling, means that other species can move into an area which is both drier and more fertile than before the alder arrived. The section of woodland a little further long the track on the left, which is a mixture of alder and birch, demonstrates this.

It is not unusual to see the woody remains of last year's cones, this year's seed-laden fruits and next year's vestigial male catkins all on the same alder branch in autumn.

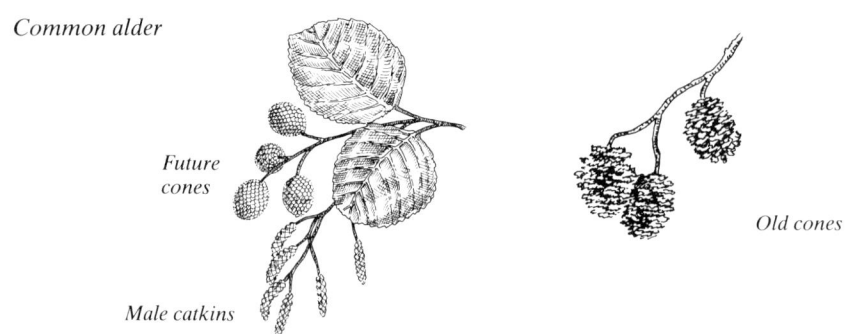

Common alder

Future cones

Male catkins

Old cones

In early spring, alders have male catkins and tiny reddish female flowers. Each heavily-veined leaf has a dent at the tip where most similar leaves are pointed and in autumn the little green fruits appear. These are like miniature conifer cones and have led to the alder being called Britain's only broad-leafed conifer. At one time, alder wood was used in the making of clogs but nowadays their major function, from man's point of view, is to hold together the banks of streams and rivers with their roots.

The sides of the track or 'drove' as it is called, are well endowed with a wide variety of flowers. At the gateway into this wood is burdock which blooms from June onwards and has thistle-like purple flowers and broad heart-shaped leaves. Already clustered around the flowers are the little hooks which are attached to the seeds. When they are ripe, these cling to any passing object and are thus dispersed to new areas. Children know these burrs well, often throwing them at each other in an effort to make them stick to clothing; they may also know burdock from the fact that an essence from the plant is used to make dandelion and burdock pop.

Burdock

Its hooked seeds cling to passing objects

There are also members of the umbellifer family growing alongside the drove. Among them may be found angelica with its many white flowers clustered into umbrella-like hemispheres which like those of its relatives, cow parsley and hog weed, are then grouped at the head of the stem. They are much loved by insects. Soldier beetles – long orange insects with black tips to their wing-cases – are found on them in July and August and can often be seen mating there. In fact soldier beetles are carnivorous and probably wait on umbellifers, such as angelica, to pounce on unwary insects visiting these attractive flowers. While the flowers are in evidence from July, the plant is easily recognisable before that by its leaves, which are similar to those of ash trees, and by the cup-like sheath around each leaf stem where it joins the main stalk. It is from the cultivated form that the candied-green cake decoration is made.

In June, too, the heavy fragrance of meadowsweet should be detected which also likes these damp areas. At first glance it is like angelica, growing to almost the same height, but its flowers are more creamy in less-ordered flowerheads, its stems are red, and its leaves more defined having a veined upper surface and light downy underneath. Meadowsweet's delightful scent led to its being used in medieval times as a floor-covering along with rushes and it is also said to have similar medicinal properties to those of aspirin.

At the end of the woodland along the field-edge is a birch tree with large bunches of tiny branches growing in clumps. These are called witches' brooms and are caused by a virus, fungus or an insect stimulating tiny buds into abnormal growth which would not normally grow at all. This freak growth, while looking odd, causes only minor harm to the tree itself.

Birch branch with witches' broom

Just before the bridge there is a gateway into which stone has been imported to strengthen the track, as this soft peaty ground is very spongy. Pieces of leather may also be seen – industrial offcuts from the local shoe industry. In the north of England, in similar situations, old conveyor-belting from pits is used.

The climb onto the bridge is quite steep. This is because the structure has been lifted well above the North Drain here so as not to impede the water flow in times of flood. Once on the bridge carefully scan the water and the banks. Mute swans should be seen and possibly the still, grey form of a heron and, if very lucky, the blue flash of a kingfisher. The backs and the wings of these birds are turquoise while their breasts and underparts are a rich almost orange chestnut. They live on fish which they catch either by waiting patiently on a perch above the water or by hovering over the surface. Then they plunge into the water, capture their prey and fly back to their perch.

If a kingfisher catches a spiny fish, e.g. bullhead or stickleback, it will beat it against its perch until dead and eat it head first lest the fins and spines catch in its throat as the fish is being swallowed.

Kingfisher killing a fish against its perch

Kingfishers nest in a burrow two to three feet long which they excavate themselves in the river bank. The eggs are round and white. Birds' eggs laid in an exposed location, such as a ledge on a sea cliff, are usually very pointed so that if disturbed they will roll in a circle and not fall over the edge and smash on the rocks below. Those of the kingfisher could hardly be less exposed and so any shaping is superfluous. Furthermore, eggs found in cup-shaped nests or laid on the ground have cryptic coloration. They are camouflaged to disguise them from the eyes of predators; if anything, eggs laid at the end of a dark tunnel need to be visible to the parent birds so as to avoid accidental breakages and thus white would be the preferred colour.

When the eggs hatch, the chicks are fed on minnows, sticklebacks and a few large insects such as dragonflies. The nest chamber is soon knee deep in old fish-bones and other debris to the extent that the parents have to wash when they emerge. The young kingfishers have to learn how to fish when they leave the nest and the adults will continue to feed them until this is accomplished.

This sort of river was once a normal part of an otter's habitat and while the otter is almost extinct in England, a few still survive on the Somerset levels and moors, one would, however, be extremely lucky to see one here. Their decline was first noticed in the early seventies when the Mammal Society looked into the records of otter hunts and discovered a serious drop in the number of 'finds' between 1957 and 1967. Further investigations pointed to the heavy use of some pesticides as being one of the major reasons for this and although these chemicals are now banned, other pressures have come to bear on the already depleted population.

Otters

Otters are now very rare and totally protected

The otter's favourite food seems to be eels, with course fish and frogs following a close second. This type of prey is easy to catch and abundant in the muddier, slow-moving lowland rivers – the sort of waterways which have become popular for water sports which create disturbances that otters cannot stand. These same rivers are maintained in a clear state by the various drainage authorities which remove bankside trees and bushes in order to allow access for machines. The North Drain is a good example of this and of the straight waterways that are so good for drainage but not for otters. Bankside cover is essential for lying up during the day and, more important still, for breeding. Fortunately some of the more enlightened authorities are clearing the bank on only one side of the river to let their dredgers in, although this action may not be in time to save the otter.

Where possible, they have moved up into the hills away from the often crowded and polluted bare-banked lowland waters, but here the streams run faster and food is more scarce and therefore able to support less otters. The network of sluggish waterways on the Somerset levels and moors was always considered to be an otter's paradise and, although declining elsewhere in England, it remained in fairly large numbers in this area. Research over the recent past, however, has shown that even here the otter population is dwindling and it could be that there are now too few otters for them ever to build up their population again.

Progressing down the drove an area is entered where peat digging has only recently finished. It has been acquired as a nature reserve by the Somerset Trust for Nature Conservation with financial help from the Nature Conservancy Council, John Paul Getty junior and the World Wildlife Fund. At the time of writing Greater Westhay Reserve is very new, and carefully designed with numerous water channels, islands and promontories to provide a range of habitats. Over 600 alder trees and almost as many willows have been planted while beds of reeds and reedmace are planned. Bird hides are to be built and a wide variety of birds are expected. Already herons and kestrels, kingfishers and reed warblers have been seen while tracks by the water's edge indicate that badgers and foxes are regular visitors.

*Chickweed.
Once eaten as salad*

The trunks of many young willows on the left have been scored or 'frayed' by the antlers of roe bucks to assist in the removal of velvet from their new antlers and also to leave scent 'signatures' behind.

This area is used by the peat extraction industry for which the moors are well known. Peat – partially decomposed compacted vegetable matter – is cut into small bricks, dried and used for burning and, to some extent, for gardens. It is a slow-burning fuel which does not give off much heat but is very fragrant.

When demand was low, peat banks were allowed to regenerate after cutting and new peat would form fairly quickly. Nowadays the demand for garden peat is much greater and huge areas are excavated, stacked, bagged and sold in garden centres, without giving the peat a chance to re-make itself.

The effects are far reaching for, in order to excavate the peat efficiently, large machines are used and the water table is lowered by pumping which dries the marshy ground. This alters the vegetation, depriving water-loving species of moisture and allowing plants preferring drier ground to invade and colonise. Although some parts of the levels and moors are saved for conservation purposes, these can be less viable due to drainage activities in the vicinity.

Hereabouts can be seen the straight vertical cuts in the soil left by the peat-cutters which slice out blocks much more rapidly than old-fashioned hand cutting and leave neat pieces to be stacked and dried ready for carting. Looking across the diggings on the left of the drove is a woodland of birch and alder and among them on both sides of the track are tall evergreen Scots pines. Although conifers, they do not grow in the typical 'pyramidal' Christmas-tree shape but tend to have a more random arrangement of branches. On the upper parts of the trunk the bark is chestnut coloured, a hue which is especially striking in the low sunlight at dawn or dusk. The blue-green needles grow in pairs and in winter two different types of cone may be seen on the same tree; tiny first-year cones on the branch tips and larger more easily recognisable green two-year-old cones which ripen in spring.

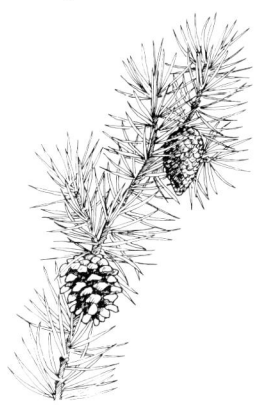

*Scots pine branch
with cones which open to
shed their seeds when ripe*

In this area teasels should be found – easily identifiable in spring by their prickly stems and backbone of spines that follow the centre of the underside of the leaf. The leaves themselves form a cup around the main stem which collects water and often small insects which, after a while, begins to smell rather foetid. In July and August the purple flowers appear in a spiny head which always looks flea-bitten and incomplete. When the flowers are finished, the head remains and persists well into winter. It is this seedhead, with its many tiny hooks, that was once used to raise the nap on newly-woven cloth. A sub-species was grown, especially in Somerset, for the sole purpose of 'teasing' cloth in this way. Some people like to grow it in their gardens to attract goldfinches which eat the seeds.

Goldfinches are beautiful little birds with red and white face patches and a black cap. On their wings is a yellow flash which becomes a golden wing stripe in flight. The red face-feathers are stiff and strong and act as guard feathers against the spines of their foodplants which include thistles and burdock as well as the non-spiky groundsel and dandelion. A twittering flock or 'charm' of goldfinches may be seen feeding here.

> *The goldfinches' happy song made it a popular bird to capture and cage during the last century. This is illegal in Britain now but many birds are still caught and caged in other European countries.*

Groundsel

Dandelion.
It takes its name from its toothed leaves – in French 'dent de lion'

Teasel.
Once used to 'tease' cloth

Turn round at the large oak tree at the corner of the woodland on the right and retrace the route.

Look out across the diggings in the wetter areas for greater reedmace (bulrushes). The most recognisable feature of this plant is its beautiful dark-brown seed-head which is formed in July but does not shed its seeds until the following February. Anyone collecting these for decoration will know to their cost how the windborne seeds suddenly spring from within the brown outer coating in a shower of white fluff.

Pass out of the peat diggings, through the reserve and back into farmland.

*Southern hawker
dragonfly*

*Flowering
bulrush
(greater
reedmace)*

*Bulrush after flowering
leaving only seed-heads*

*Ruddy darter
dragonfly*

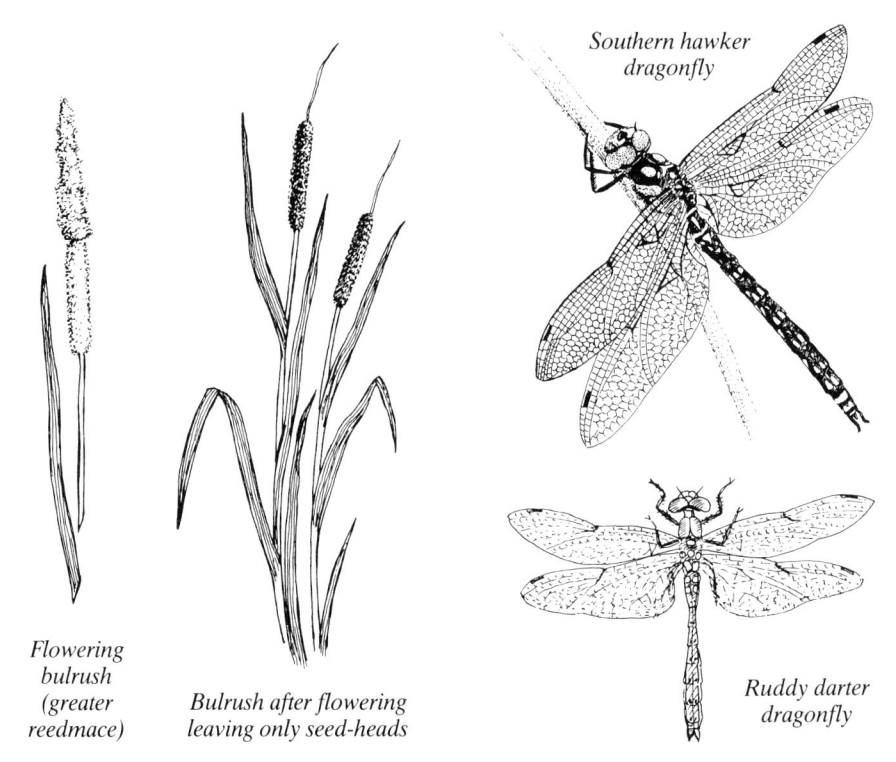

The ten acre lake on the left is part of the Greater Westhay Reserve and is an area where peat extraction is complete. Already the water is in use by several species and coots at least should be seen. A flock of goosanders, diving ducks with narrow bills, have been observed here in winter while a hen harrier has been spotted on more than one occasion.

The meadows here are frequently damp and sometimes flood in winter. The spiky groups of rushes among the grass are indicators of wet soil and the deep rhynes on either side of the drove are important to help drain the water from the land. They are also used as 'wet fences' for, being both deep and water-logged, they prevent farm animals from straying. Although they may appear black and glossy in winter, these watercourses teem with life in the summer months.

Alongside them may grow irises (yellow flags) with their beautiful and brilliant yellow flowers in May and June. Later in the year, the heavy bright-green pointed seed pods appear. Moorhens skulk in the rhyne bottoms and even nest in their undergrowth and often the silent stealthy heron will fish the banks. Dragonflies and damsel flies frequent this area. The dragonfly is the bigger of the two and holds its wings outspread when at rest while the damsel fly holds its wings together down its back. Dragonflies are very helicopter-like and their whirring wings make an audible rustle in flight as they hunt up and down these waterways.

The most likely dragonfly to be found here is the large southern hawker. Also noticeable may be the stubbier-bodied ruddy darter, a less common brilliant-red dragonfly. Look, too, for red damsel flies, particularly in September when they can frequently be found resting on rocks and gates, possibly in order to obtain the heat these perches have absorbed from the sun.

In the fields on the left may be spotted both peewits (lapwings) – those apparently black and white birds with crests – and curlews, with the long down-curved bill and mournful cry. Hares may be observed from the shelter of the drove if the watcher is quiet. They are the high-speed racers of British mammals and even at slow speeds will cover three metres in a single bound. Hares, except for being larger, appear similar to rabbits but differ in almost every other way. They live entirely above ground, relying on camouflage or speed to escape from danger. They make small nests (forms) in the grass and will sit absolutely still in these until almost trod upon. They then

Peewits (lapwings) in summer. Their apparently black wings are in fact a beautiful dark green

spring up at great speed, clearing the ground in enormous leaps and jumping hedges and bramble thickets in their efforts to get away. Although, by and large, they live solitary lives, hares are seen together at mating time in spring. The young (leverets) are not born blind and naked like baby rabbits but are fully furred and ready to run. The mother disperses them in a number of individual forms which she visits to allow them to suckle. If one of the leverets is discovered by a predator, the others have a chance of escape.

In some of the fields metal objects can be seen from which a hose-pipe snakes down into a nearby rhyne. These are drinking facilities for cattle. In attempting to drink they press down on a bar which operates a pump, drawing up their own water from the ditch. This prevents the animals trying to reach the water in the bottom of the rhyne and becoming stuck in the mud or perhaps escaping from the field.

Return to the starting point.

Hare

March is a good time to look out for hares

LITTON

An arm of Lower Litton Reservoir

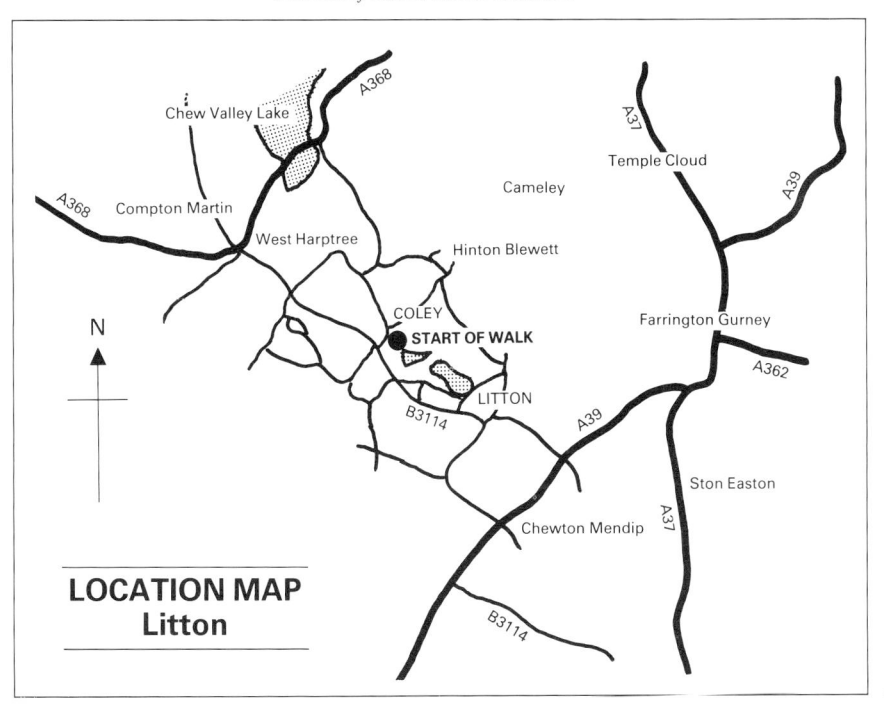

**LOCATION MAP
Litton**

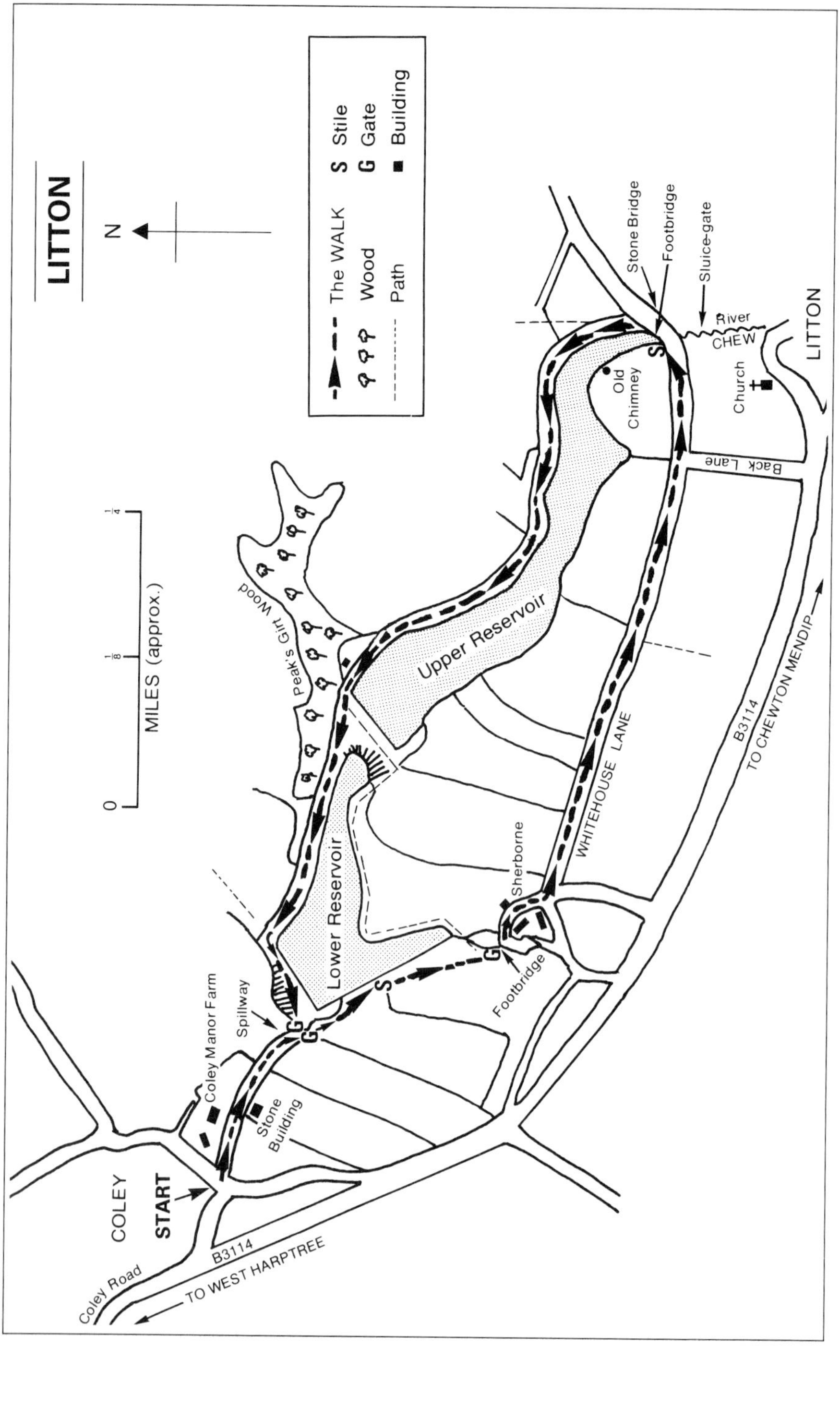
LITTON
N
The WALK
Wood
Path
S Stile
G Gate
Building
MILES (approx.)
0
1/8
1/4
Peak's Girt Wood
Upper Reservoir
Lower Reservoir
Stone Bridge
Footbridge
Sluice-gate
River CHEW
LITTON
Old Chimney
Church
Back Lane
WHITEHOUSE LANE
B3114
TO CHEWTON MENDIP
Sherborne
Footbridge
Spillway
Coley Manor Farm
Stone Building
COLEY
START
Coley Road
B3114
TO WEST HARPTREE

LITTON

Grid Ref. OS 182 (1:50 000) 583 557   Approx. 2 miles

The two Litton reservoirs are lakes hidden by folds in the Mendip hills and form the centrepiece of this walk of almost two miles. They straddle the Avon and Somerset border and, though the walk starts in Somerset, it passes into Avon and then back into Somerset once more. The route is fairly flat and dry in all but the wettest weather and it is fairly sheltered too. The trees and birds certainly make the journey worthwhile.

The walk starts in the hamlet of Coley and proceeds up the access track to the reservoirs. Pass a farm on the left and a large stone building on the right and continue towards the cattle-grid. Turn right here, climb the rail fence to the left of the leftmost of the two metal gates and follow the fence around to the left alongside the spillway.

In the right-hand edge of the field is a large, old, pollarded ash – the centre of which appears to be completely hollow. Before the hollow area becomes so large, such trees are used extensively by various species of birds. The first may be a species of woodpecker which actually creates the entrance and clears out a chamber inside for its nest, or possibly a starling which makes use of an existing weakness left by a broken branch. An increase in the hole size could allow an owl to enter and rear its brood, and both the little owl and the tawny owl will use such locations. It is quite likely, though, that the site will eventually become uninhabitable for birds as the tree continues to rot down to the base. Large mammals will then take over. I have found fox dens (earths), with one or two additional underground entrances, centred on such a hollow tree. Badgers may sometimes use them as 'day nests' which are lying-up places

Vixen with cubs

Foxes are often easier to see in towns than in the country

located away from the main sett in hidden sites. The badger will bring in large quantities of dry grass and leaves and use the nest either for lying up during the day or, more commonly, for resting part-way through the night. Having eaten a good meal of earthworms – its favourite food – the badger will often have an after-dinner nap in such a day nest rather than returning to the sett.

The reservoirs here have been refurbished and the area between the fence and the spillway has been planted with shrubs. Holly will be seen here, amongst other species, in black-wire guards to prevent them being damaged by rabbits for, when the weather is cold and food is difficult to find, these mammals will eat the bark from small trees and often kill them as a result. The rabbit's mouth is specially designed to do this as it has a split upper-lip which enables the animal to get its teeth close to the trunk and remove the bark efficiently without damage to itself. Ultimately the rabbit has the edge on the forester as, in very cold weather when there is deep snow, the raised ground level enables it to reach above the rabbit guard and remove the bark higher up the tree or even the leading shoot from the top of the stem!

> *The rabbit's front incisors grow continually to make up for hard wear. If fed only soft food and with nothing hard to chew, its teeth would continue to grow, eventually curling round and becoming useless, causing the rabbit to die of starvation.*

Cross the double stile.

The hedge on the left contains a wide variety of shrubby species and this is indicative of its great age. Field maple is here – an often neglected tree. Its leaves are five-lobed like the leaf on the Canadian emblem and, in autumn, they turn to a magnificent gold. The fruits are winged, like those of sycamore, but joined in pairs horizontally unlike the sycamore's 'V' shape. The field maple is a lover of chalk and limestone but tends to do better in the south-east rather than here where it rarely attains more than shrub size. In Kent, for example, there are records of field maples reaching almost 80 feet.

Hawthorn (quickthorn) is easy to spot in that it has shortish straight thorns. Its leaves sprout fairly early in spring and for a week or so roadside hawthorn hedges look beautiful with just a haze of light-green. Once they emerge fully, the leaves are three- or five-lobed and are followed in May by masses of scented white blossom – hence may-blossom. The round dull-red fruits (haws) stand out in autumn once the leaves have fallen giving the small hawthorn trees and hedges a reddish appearance. They are much favoured by small birds, particularly members of the thrush family – such as the winter-migrants fieldfare and redwing – and enjoyed, too, by small mammals which climb the trees to harvest them. Strangely enough, bank voles enjoy the flesh and discard the stones whilst woodmice throw away the fruit to reach the pip.

Look out for the red twigs and oval pointed leaves of dogwood. This species also has white flowers in spring and black berries in autumn. As it thrives on chalk and limestone ground, the dogwood presents a problem to conservationists by invading downland. If there are no sheep or rabbits present to keep it in check, the shrub will rapidly take over, suckering vigorously.

On the left on the other side of the hedge is an arm of the reservoir containing three plants which remain in their skeletal form well into winter. In the wetter, marshy areas are reeds; the tallest grass found in Britain, and grown specifically in East Anglia for thatching. A large bed of reeds looks delightful on a breezy day as the wind ripples through the tall stems in waves, causing them to ebb and flow in a variety of buffs, beiges and browns. They provide nesting places for the reed warbler – a bird with buff underparts, a light-brown back, and a rather repetitive song.

The reed warbler is a victim of the parasitic cuckoo. It lays an egg in its hosts' nest and removes one of the eggs relying on the newly-hatched cuckoo to tip out the remainder and leaving the parent warblers to rear their large foster fledgling.

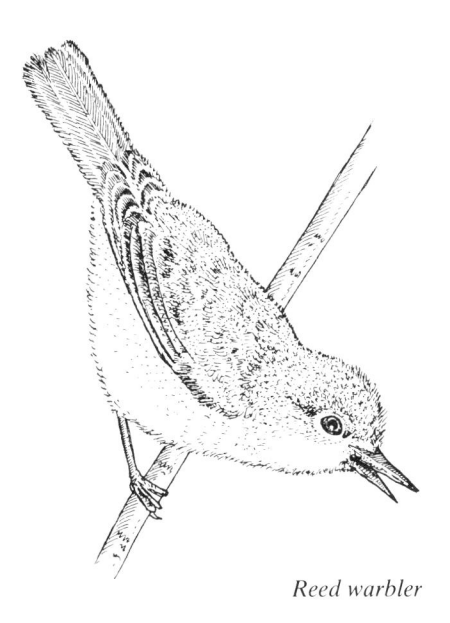

Reed warbler

Rosebay willowherb grows here too: a tall plant which, en masse in summer, makes a brilliant-purple splash of colour. It has a tall cluster of four-petalled flowers giving way to seeds on cottony plumes which are spread generously on a windy day. Once rare, it began to spread in the middle of the last century possibly as a result of the railway boom, for it is a coloniser of recently-burned ground and is common on railway embankments which are frequently fired to curtail the vegetation. It did well during World War II and rapidly moved into bomb-sites in London and other cities so that, nowadays, it can be found almost anywhere in Britain.

Thirdly, there is a nettlebed here. The green-flowered stinging nettle, which is familiar to just about everyone, is the food plant of the caterpillars of the vanessid group of butterflies which includes such beautiful insects as the small tortoiseshell, the peacock and the red admiral.

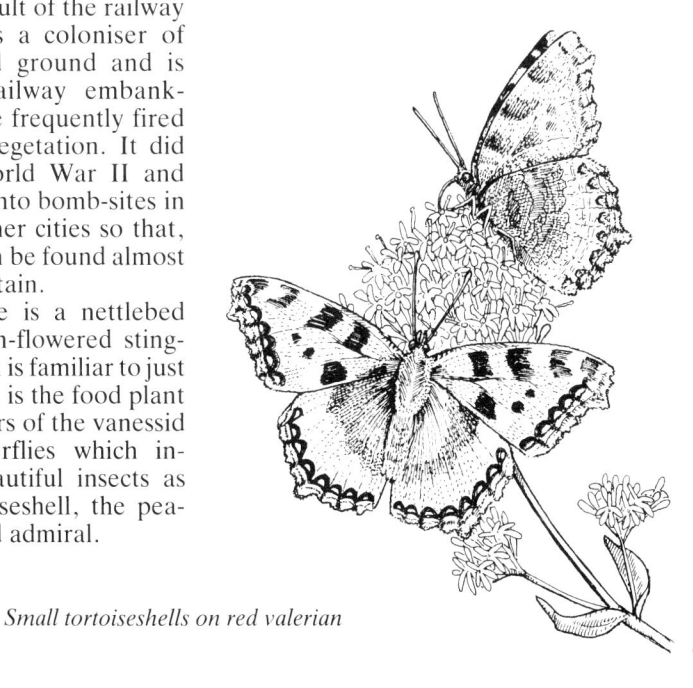

Small tortoiseshells on red valerian

Peacock
It has eyes on its wings like those on the bird

Red admiral

Turn left over a stile, cross the footbridge and climb the rise between the two houses. Look out for the Scots pine on the left and the beech hedge atop the wall on the right. Turn left at the top into Whitehouse Lane just past the no-through-road sign on the left.

Almost opposite the sign, beside the field entrance, is a double step which has been constructed for horses to jump down. Called a quarry jump, it is a type of obstacle found on cross-country courses such as those held at Badminton, Goucestershire each year.

This is a typical English country lane, running between hedgerows and with fields on either side. Keep a look out for the runways of foxes and badgers through the hedges. These are rarely opposite one another across the road but tend to be slightly offset. If there is mud, the badger's broad, flat-footed, five-toed track may be seen or the fox's dainty four-toed track – its front claws almost touching and a distinct cross visible between the pads. (See pages 118–119 for illustrations of animal tracks.) There may be hair too, caught on barbed wire or thorns. Badger hairs are coarse and black in the middle with white tips while those of the fox are brown or ginger and much finer. (See page 116.)

Holly is abundant in the hedge on the left. It has small white flowers in May but as the trees are either male or female, only the latter has the well-known, bright-red berries, although not produced every year. The dark-green waxy leaves are able to survive even frosty weather and can stay on the plant for up to four years. Generally they are only spiky low down on the tree where they are in danger of being browsed. Higher up, the leaves have no spikes and it is said that they used to be collected to feed stock, notably in the north.

Many hedgerow flowers can be seen along this lane and red campion, cow parsley and white deadnettle with its soft, green leaves without a sting, should be found. Cow parsley is one of the earliest flowering members of the umbellifer family, its prolific white blooms giving rise to its country name of 'Queen Anne's lace'. On the verge opposite the turning on the right, three horse-chestnut trees have been planted and their hoof-printed leaf scars are easy to see. Hanging over the stream on the left is a branch of an ash tree bearing polypody ferns. These are fond of moist places and enjoy life in the warm, wet south-west shunning the east of Britain entirely. (See illustration on page 114).

Here, on the right, can be seen Litton Church tower and the village itself is no distance away. Chew River has been penned upstream and tumbles noisily over the sluice-gates. To find a stream like this on Mendip is unusual for most water quickly finds its way underground seeping through cracks in the limestone to create caves and reappearing as resurgences at places like Wookey Hole and Cheddar. It is no wonder that full use was made of the running water in years gone by.

Just before the stone road-bridge, go over the barred stile on the left, cross the footbridge and follow the path around the side of the reservoir.

This is the Upper Litton Reservoir which was constructed in 1850, four years after the completion of the lower one. They were both built as compensation reservoirs so that when Bristol Waterworks Company took its supplies from the spring at Chewton Mendip, those living downstream would not be deprived of water. The river now runs on into Chew Valley Lake.

On the opposite bank, an interesting collection of trees are reflected when the water is still. There are oaks, gaunt skeletons with elbows in winter; larches, the only deciduous conifer; ash; and spruce, which keep their leaves throughout the year. The larch is a beautiful tree with its crooked tops. In spring its needles appear in a delicate shade of green which looks outstanding when set against a background of dark-foliaged spruce trees. At this time, too, it has small pink flowers. The needles turn a rusty-gold in autumn and fall to cover the whole floor of a larch plantation with the same rich colour.

Beside them are the remains of an ivy-clad chimney with a square stone base and brick thereafter. It probably marks the site of one of several mills, used for agricultural purposes, which were located alongside the fast-flowing Chew before the reservoir was constructed.

Just past the second stile on the right of the path a spindle tree will be found. This species of tree often goes unnoticed, growing no taller than 15 feet. It has green flowers in spring but comes into its full glory in autumn when it produces shocking-pink fruit capsules, divided into four lobes which split to reveal the orange flesh inside, covering a yellow seed. The fruit is as delightful for its shape – resembling a miniature lantern – as for its colour. The tree takes its name from the use of its wood in the making of hand-spindles for wool-spinning in times past. The hard, white splinter-free wood has ideal properties for such a use.

Larch flowers

Male

Female

> Dutch elm disease killed about 600,000 trees between 1968 and 1971 of the 18 million elms in southern England.

Elm bark beetle galleries

Eggs are laid in the central area and the larvae burrow outwards forming 'galleries' – which are revealed when the bark is shed

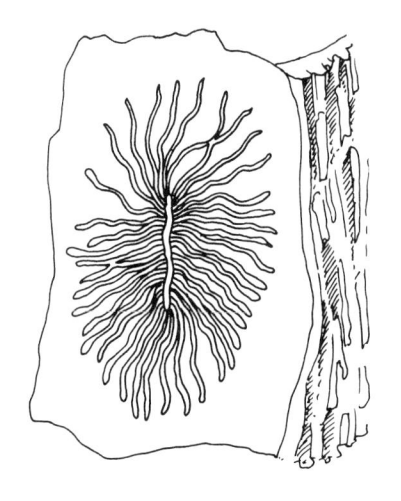

A little further along, on the left-hand side, are some young elms whose leaves are rough to the touch. Notice, too, that the two sides of the leaf do not meet in the same place on the stalk. Dutch elm disease killed many mature trees in this area and the remains of one will be passed shortly on the right. In many places young elms are thriving and they continue to grow until they give up the sappy skin of youth and take on the proper bark of the adult elm. At this point the ambrosia beetle can make its galleries under the bark (these should be able to be seen on one of the trees here) and brings with it a fungus which, in turn, kills the layer of wood immediately beneath the bark which contains the veins to carry food throughout the tree. Once this wood is destroyed, the whole tree dies.

Listen out for warblers here during the summer months as two species in particular are easy to identify by their song. The first is the chiff-chaff – which looks remarkably like the willow warbler and even has similarities to the reed warbler. Its song is a giveaway though, for it repeats 'chiff-chaff, chiff-chaff, chiff-chaff' almost all the time. At close quarters it can be caught making a quiet churring sound to itself. The willow warbler arrives a month later, in mid-April, having flown over 2,000 miles from tropical Africa. Its song is a melodic cadence which descends the scale and fades away. Strangely enough while the chiff-chaff rears only one brood, the busy willow warbler with a month less for the task, manages to bring off two.

As the house is passed, look back across the garden where a tall dark blue-green tree stands. This is an evergreen holm oak which has dense foliage to which new leaves are added in June. The acorn cup forms up the side of the acorn so that up to three-quarters of the seed is enclosed.

The dam for the top reservoir has now been reached and there are, on the downstream side, special hollow concrete blocks designed to provide a hard surface, which disappear among the grass, making it possible to mow over them. This type of block was designed in the late sixties for temporary car parking and infrequently-used accesses in the countryside so that the general grass cover is maintained and not ruined by vehicle tracks in the soil.

At the bottom of the hill, beside the top of the lower reservoir is an oak tree which has been neatly trimmed and treated to prevent fungal attack. Opposite it will be found a member of the fir family. Many firs are readily identified by the fruity smell the needles emit when they are crushed. An import from North America, they flower in spring and produce seed-bearing cones in autumn.

A section of water immediately below the upper dam has been cordoned off with a net. This area is used for fish-rearing by the Bristol Waterworks Company's fishery section. A number of water birds collect on both this and the upper reservoir. The most common species likely to be seen is the coot. This is a black bird with a white bill and a white forehead or frontal shield. It lives in large flocks in winter but tends to be very territorial and quarrelsome for the rest of the year. It does not have webbed-feet but lobes alongside each of its toes which broadens them to help it swim.

> *Coots have some difficulty in taking off and have to patter along the surface of the water in order to become airborne. This limits the size of pond they can inhabit.*

Although they are sometimes found on the same water, the related moorhen takes up residence on smaller ponds shunned by the coot. By contrast, the black moorhen has a red bill and frontal shield, and a white flash on its upright tail which jerks as it swims. This bird is more retiring than the coot, diving out of sight and into cover provided by overhanging vegetation. Both may build nests in conspicuous places which are often raided by predators as a consequence. Young coots are black and fluffy with ginger heads and, on leaving the nest, become independent after only about eight weeks.

The moorhen has a white flash on its upright tail and a red frontal shield

The coot has a white frontal shield and no apparent tail

Apart from mallard, the other species of duck likely to be seen in any numbers is the tufted duck. The drake is black with a white side-flash at the waterline and an almost dark-blue beak. He has a crest on his head from which the bird takes its name. The female is dark brown with a smaller crest. Unlike the mallard, which is a dabbling duck, the tufty is a freshwater diving duck living almost exclusively on small animal life which it hunts during its dives. When it bobs to the surface the oil from the preen gland, with which its feathers are liberally coated, drives off the water like silver beads of mercury, thus preventing the duck from becoming waterlogged and either drowning or dying of cold.

Male

Tufted duck

Walk across the dam and pass through the wicket gate to the left of the cattle-grid and return to the starting point.

The pied wagtail with its characteristic waving tail often lives around buildings. As its name suggests, it is black and white

Female

Pied wagtail

Grey wagtails may also be seen for they are fond of water. They have a light-grey back (hence their name) and a yellow breast and belly which often causes them to be confused with the much yellower, and less common, yellow wagtail

KING'S CASTLE, WELLS

'The Warren' where rabbits were probably once kept as a living larder

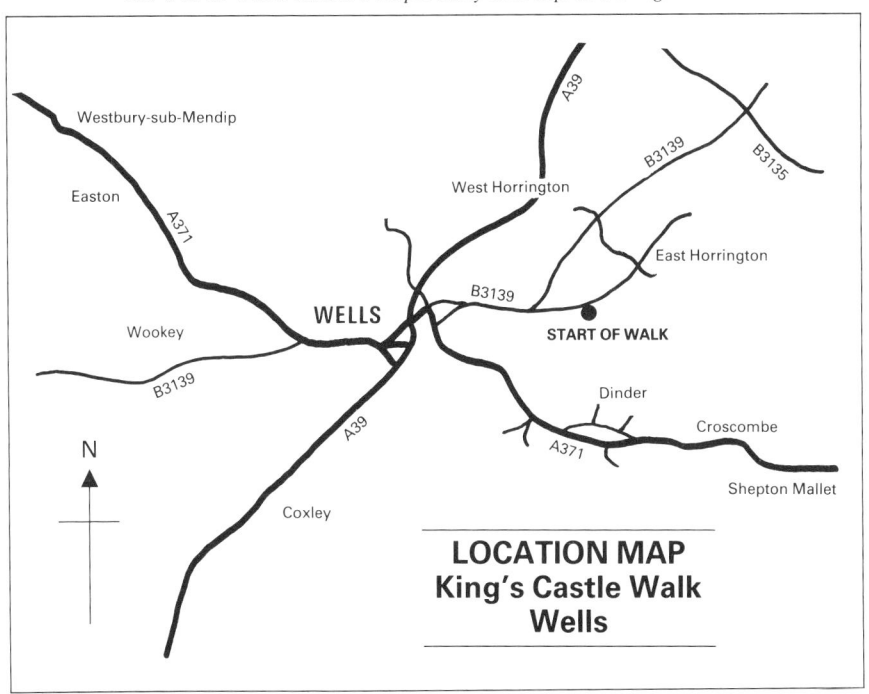

**LOCATION MAP
King's Castle Walk
Wells**

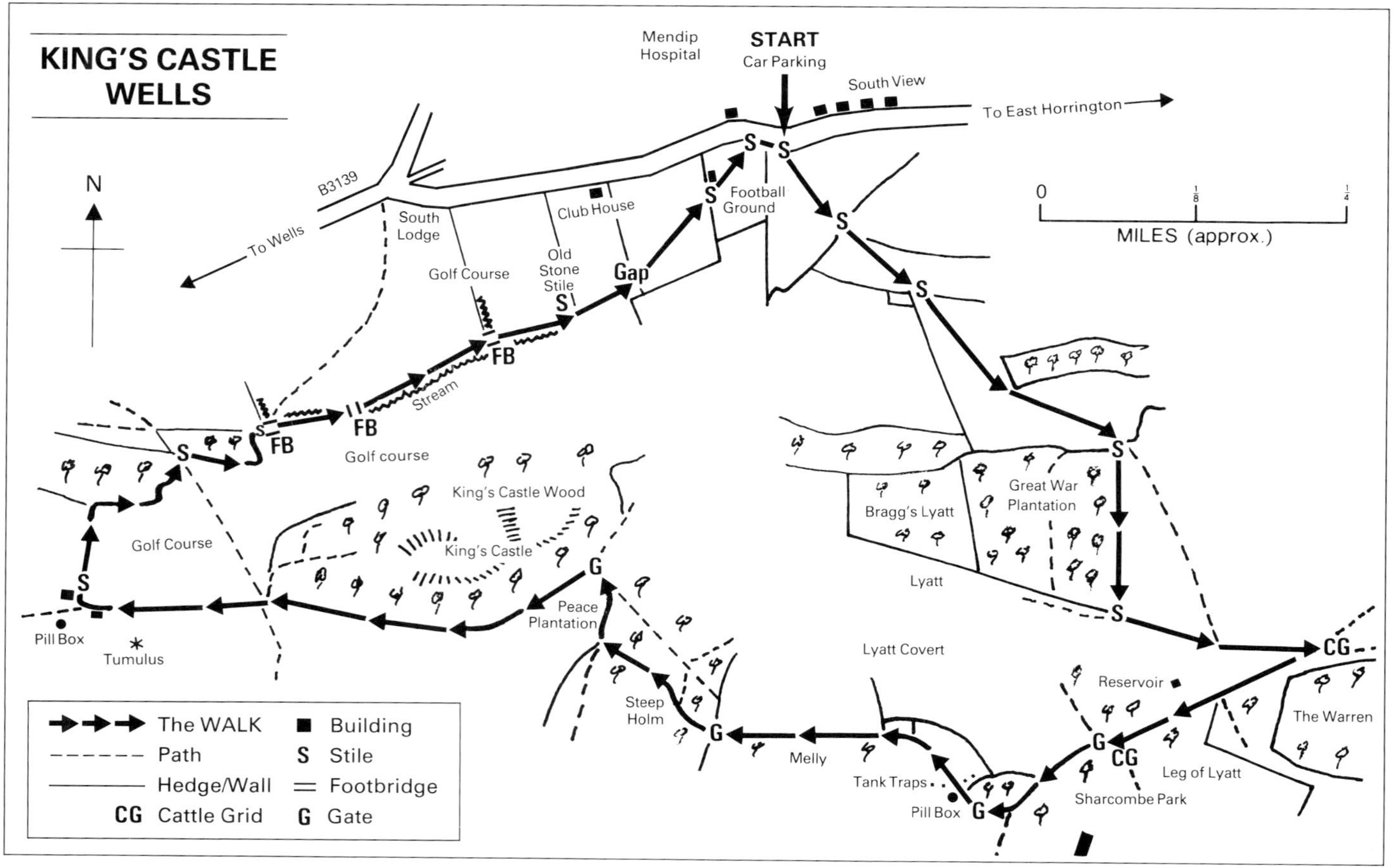
KING'S CASTLE
WELLS
N
Mendip Hospital
START
Car Parking
South View
To East Horrington
B3139
To Wells
South Lodge
Club House
Football Ground
Golf Course
Old Stone Stile
Gap
FB
Stream
Golf course
S
King's Castle Wood
King's Castle
Golf Course
Pill Box
Tumulus
Peace Plantation
G
Steep Holm
Melly
Tank Traps
Pill Box
Sharcombe Park
CG
Leg of Lyatt
Reservoir
The Warren
Lyatt Covert
Lyatt
Bragg's Lyatt
Great War Plantation
0
1/8
1/4
MILES (approx.)
The WALK
Path
Hedge/Wall
CG Cattle Grid
Building
S Stile
Footbridge
G Gate

KING'S CASTLE, WELLS

Grid Ref. OS 182 (1:50 000) 573 463   Approx. 2¾ miles

The route of this walk passes through parkland and plantation, climbing up through fields to look over Mendip and to the Somerset Levels. The return section has a distinctly sporting feel as it crosses a golf course and playing fields. In the period between planning the route and writing the text for this walk, the Somerset Trust for Nature Conservation purchased King's Castle Wood as a nature reserve. The walk is largely dry although one or two sections, especially around Peace Plantation, can be muddy and slippery.

Take the B3139 Frome road from Wells. Turn right about a mile along (at Mendip Hospital) towards East Horrington. After less than half a mile, there is a large 'H' sign (rear access to the hospital). Slightly beyond on the right where the road bends to the left the walk starts at the gate/stile.

Park carefully without causing an obstruction and climb over the stile. Cross the field walking towards two large ash trees and the gate beyond with a railed style to one side.

Like many of the trees on this walk, the ash here are showing signs of their age. They have lost a number of boughs and often this spells the beginning of the end for a tree, as water gets into the main trunk and begins to rot the wood. In specimens as large as this, such an end will be a long time coming and meanwhile many plants and animals can take advantage of the weakness. Woodpeckers drill holes into the wood, mainly in search of food but also to create a nest chamber in the breeding season. These will frequently be commandeered by starlings in future years. Bats will seek holes in the tree for roosting and tits will take advantage of any small cavities in which to build nests. Fungi quickly take hold and sometimes quite unexpected plants such as the elder which can be seen here. A seed was probably deposited by a bird – possibly a starling, as they feast on elderberries in autumn – and the plant began to grow. No doubt this is a rather inhospitable site when the weather is hot and dry, but it does have the advantage of being safely out of reach of browsing animals.

> *The bat which most commonly uses a tree roost is the noctule. A sign that a hole is occupied is a dark streak on the tree trunk below the entrance. But they are no match for starlings who have been known to evict and even kill these bats living in a hole that the birds wish to occupy.*

Climb the style and walk along the old track to the first ash tree from where the path strikes off across the field down towards the wooden pens in the right-hand hedge and the spreading oak above them.

Below, a cattle grid has been set into the fence line. Such grids are a stockproof method of allowing easy access for vehicles and this would appear to be a route used frequently by the farmer when animals are in the fields. This location is an unusual one in that cattle grids are normally only used on or beside roads as they are an expensive alternative to ordinary field gates. Hedgehogs have been known to fall into the pit beneath and been unable to escape. The Hedgehog Protection Society, run by Major Adrian Coles, has been campaigning for some time for small ramps to be installed in every grid to enable trapped animals to get out.

> *Hedgehogs live a daring life. On reaching a drop, they may confidently cast themselves into the abyss, relying of their springy spines to cushion the fall. Sadly, apart from cattle grids, many fall into swimming pools and steep-sided garden ponds. Unable to climb out they eventually drown.*

Climb the double-rail stile to the left of the pens before going up the hill passing the large and very fine pedunculate oak on the way.

Oaks are well known for the number of insect species they support and it is always fascinating to shake a leafy branch over an old sheet or an inverted open umbrella. A surprising number of creepy-crawlies will tumble off which are readily identifiable with a good field guide. It is quite plain why flocks of tits and other insectivorous birds spend so much time picking carefully through the foliage of these trees. This oak, in particular, is more obvious in the life it supports. Like the ash which supported the elder seen earlier, this tree has fronds of brambles dangling from a small bush growing in its crown while the coolness of its shady interior provides perfect conditions for the common polypody fern. In spite of appearances, this fern is not a parasite but lives on the nutrients which collect in the damp and fissured bark of trees. In dry summers, its leaves brown and wither but the plant becomes surprisingly verdant when a wet period follows.

The path clips the top corner of the mixed plantation of spruce and ash which protrudes into the field. Often in situations like this, the faster growing coniferous softwoods are used as a nurse to shelter hardwood species like the ash encouraging them to grow tall and straight, thus adding value to the resultant timber.

This wood is surrounded by a dense guard of bramble through which badger tunnels and deer paths may be seen. Scabious grows along this hedgerow and, although often thought of as a flower of high summer, it is surprising how it persists well into autumn, adding a splash of colour to a damp countryside on dour days.

Walk over the brow of the hill towards the tall ash trees in the corner of the wood.

To the left is the filled remains of a field pond – one of the unfortunate signs of modern agriculture which has deprived so many amphibians and insects of suitable habitats. The materials used for infilling include bricks and stones, and it would also seem that some garden escapees were imported at the same time for yellow poppies grow here along with buttercups and stinging nettles – typical weeds of disturbed ground. There are rushes too which indicate that the pond area is still quite damp.

Scabious

Its flowers persist well into autumn

The flower and leaves of dogwood

At the wood, climb over the metal-railed stile and walk between the fence and the woodland edge.

Known as the Great War Plantation, it contains a great mixture of species. There is a delightful variety of shrubs growing alongside the path which includes hazel, field maple, dogwood, bramble and hawthorn. Its name would suggest that the trees in this wood were planted during or just after World War I, a time when so many of our woods were felled to provide timber for the war effort. It was largely as a result of the need to carry out extensive planting to replace these trees that the Forestry Commission was established in 1919. Take care when walking alongside the barbed-wire fence and look out particularly for the runs of badgers and deer. Where these pass under or through the fence, tufts of animal hair caught on the barbs should be found.

The coarse guard hairs from the back of the badger would be trapped on the bottom strand of wire while roe deer would have left their back hair on the second strand. Hairs from their stomachs may be seen on the bottom wire where they have passed between the two. (See page 116 for illustrations.)

> *Some fences are no match for badgers. They can scramble over walls, push their way under wire netting and have been known to batter a hole through a larch lap fence erected across one of their traditional paths.*

On reaching the end of the wood, climb over the stile passing through festoons of traveller's joy whose long grey hairy plumes of windborne seeds give it the name of 'old man's beard'.

Turn left following the edge of the field until it runs to a point and joins a track. Turn sharp right along this and down the opposite side of the triangular field.

Just over the wall here is an area called The Warren. This is most probably the remains of a managed warren – a secure walled enclosure with mounds of soil for the inhabitants to burrow into – where rabbits were kept as a 'living larder'. Managed warrens originated in about the twelfth century and were a popular method of ensuring a supply of fresh meat. From the eighteenth century onwards, however, the agricultural revolution enabled landowners to concentrate on larger stock.

Looking over towards the stile that was crossed to enter this field, Pen Hill mast is visible in the distance. Rising to a height of 990 feet (305 metres) its appearance can vary enormously depending upon the prevailing weather conditions. I saw it on one occasion when the clouds were heavy around its base and yet the upper white structure was in full sunlight which gave it the appearance of a Saturn rocket climbing powerfully into space.

The track soon drops down a fairly steep slope.

Here, the surface of the track has been metalled to help reduce the erosion from which ordinary stone paths suffer. A track seriously eroded in this way will be seen a little farther along the walk. The limestone wall on the left provides a home for a number of plants typical of this situation, among them being ivy-leaved toadflax and maidenhair spleenwort. The former belongs to the figwort family, as does the snapdragon, and the flowers of the two species have some similarities while, as its name suggests, its leaves are very distinctly like those of ivy. Maidenhair spleenwort is a wall-growing fern with shiny black stalks to its fronds along which are small dark-green paired leaflets – it is easily recognised here.

Do NOT turn left through the iron gate with the cattle grid into Sharcombe Park but bear right continuing on the track under the spreading limbs of some beautiful, tall beech trees. After a short distance pass through a gate (normally open) and walk down the hill where water has scoured away the surface of the track to reveal the underlying bedrock.

At the end of the wood, bear round to the right and past the door in the wall with the animal run beneath.

There are remnants of World War II here: a pill box on the left and some large concrete tank traps on the right. Such fortifications were often placed on vulnerable routes or near natural strongholds in case of an invasion of enemy forces.

Follow the track up through the trees and the cutting in the rocks and into the field at the top. Continue straight across the field and, as you come over the hump, a wicket gate will be seen on the far side, through which the path passes.

Grey squirrels inhabit the woodland which clothes the escarpment here. They are much more terrestrial than the native red squirrel, which they have displaced, and spend a good deal of autumn cacheing food by burying it in the woods and field edges.

One theory for the replacement of red squirrels by greys is that the latter descend from the trees to dig up their larders and to forage generally for food under the trees when the cold weather arrives. The red is a light, dainty animal which remains in the tree-tops foraging for food at the very tips of quite slender twigs which would not support its larger more robust grey cousin. The really hungry time for red squirrels, though, is in the late spring and early summer when they come down to the ground in search of food. If they are the only squirrel species in the wood, then there should be plenty of food available, but when there are greys, these will have spent the winter cleaning up, leaving nothing for the later-coming reds.

There is a badgers' sett along the woodland edge here – a typical site for these animals on a steep and fairly undisturbed slope. A few holes extend into the field though, and these can bring the wrath of farmers down on badgers, especially if the field is an arable one where machinery may fall into the holes and get stuck.

Badgers

Badgers can be a nuisance to farmers when they extend their excavations into fields

Pass through the wicket gate to an area of new tree planting.

Each sapling in this plantation is in the now familiar tree guard which acts like a greenhouse to protect it and stimulate growth. When first invented these guards were bright and white but, because they were so conspicuous in the countryside, they are now manufactured in more discreet colours. One of their advantages is that they curtail damage to the trees caused by deer. This area is heavily used by roe and there are distinct signs of their presence. Well-worn paths run through the trees and under the wire fences and, in one place, a battered and partly debarked sapling shows where a buck has used the tree to leave traces of scent from glands situated on its forehead. The path follows the edge of the plantation past a number of field maples. These specimens have grown unusually tall, for they are generally a woodland species and fairly restricted in size. Their leaves take on delightful colours in autumn.

> *It is critical to keep deer away from young trees. Roe deer are quite small and once the sapling reaches about 3 feet, the leading shoot is out of reach. Foresters mind less about the topiary which the deer create with the side branches as long as the main stem remains undamaged.*

Pass through a gate and turn left keeping the wood to the right.

Field maple – leaves and seeds

The leaves take on a delightful colour in autumn

This south-facing woodland fringe is excellent for butterflies. Gatekeepers and speckled woods may be seen flitting along the hedgerows and feeding particularly on bramble flowers in high summer.

There are good views from this track especially across the fields in the valley to Glastonbury Tor. The wood on the right is called King's Castle and is owned by the Somerset Trust for Nature Conservation. The name appears to refer to an Iron-Age hillfort, faint traces of which can still be seen in the wood itself.

Male

Gatekeeper butterflies

Female

Male

Female

Speckled wood butterflies

Continue along the track for some way until some stone buildings are reached on the right and turn right just before them.

These appear to have been redundant farm buildings such as old barns which no longer fitted in with modern farming practices. They may have been too small, or their doorways too low to admit modern machinery, or may simply have been in the wrong place. Sometimes such buildings are converted into rural workshops to create opportunities for local employment whilst others, such as these, are turned into houses to provide substantial homes.

Cross the stile onto the golf course and follow the path very carefully – there is a possibility of being hit by a golf-ball! (The club has marked the path in many places by painting black arrows on rocks along the way.) Walk in a straight line to the large larch at the edge of the trees. Turn right along the woodland edge and then left down the hill beside the fence. Follow the fence to its end and cross the stile.

Halfway across the field via the well-defined path turn sharp right towards the stile/footbridge in the hedge. After the stile, follow the sign for East Horrington on the right, NOT the path signposted to Knapp Hill. Cross over the wooden footbridge and follow the stream and hedge-line on the right.

Golf courses like this can be good habitats as parts of them receive little disturbance. The hedgerows are good nesting areas for birds and the roughs are loved by small mammals who can tunnel through the grass tussocks. The well-fertilised fairways and greens contain plenty of earthworms and the short grass makes them easy to grab when they come out to feed at night. Hedgehogs, in particular, spend a lot of time foraging on golf courses.

Keep following the hedge (crossing another wooden footbridge) and then the remnants of it, past the stone stile standing in solitary splendour. Trace the dip in the ground (the course of the old ditch), cross the open area and turn left at the hedge.

Turn right through a gap into the sports field making for the right-hand corner of the white building where a stile will be found. Cross to the far left corner of the football field where there is a gate and stile. Climb the stile and turn right to get back to where the walk started.

The hedgehog often forages on golf courses (Drawing: Mo Tingey)

BLACK DOWN

The triangulation point at the top of Black Down at 1,068 feet

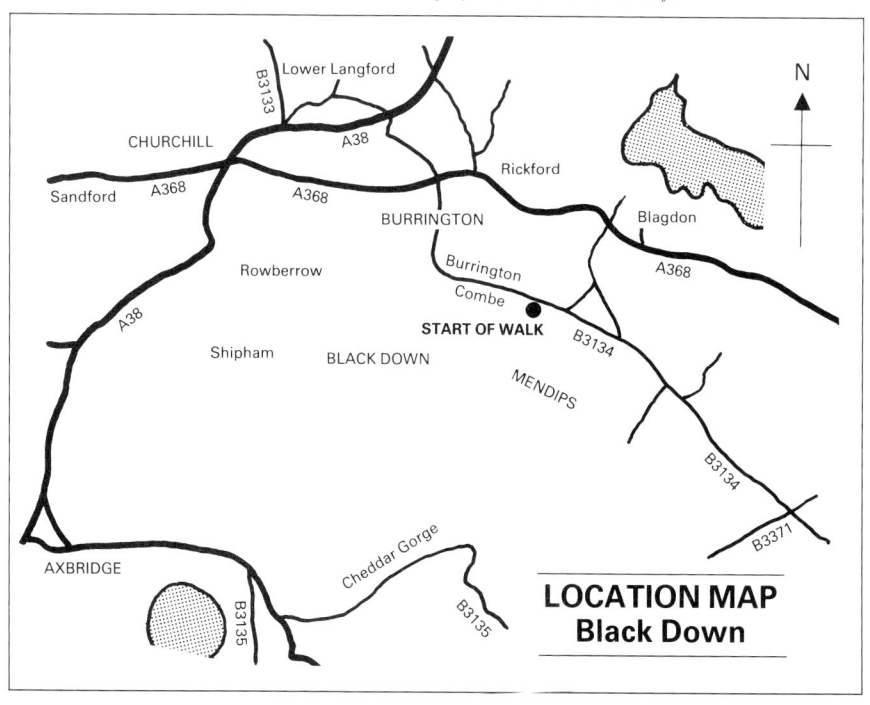

**LOCATION MAP
Black Down**

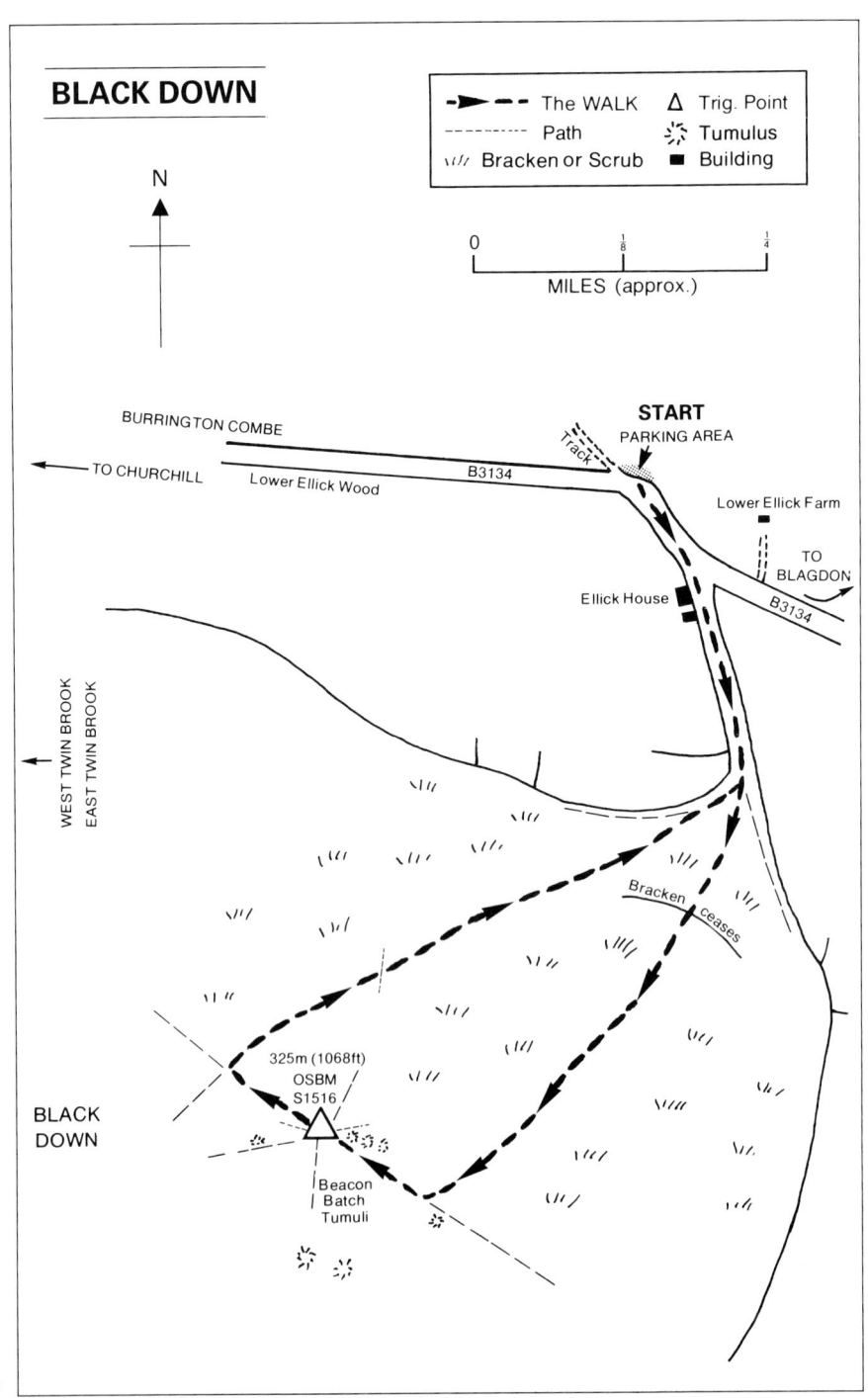

BLACK DOWN

Legend:
- The WALK
- Path
- Bracken or Scrub
- △ Trig. Point
- Tumulus
- ■ Building

Scale: 0 — 1/8 — 1/4 MILES (approx.)

N ↑

START — PARKING AREA

BURRINGTON COMBE
TO CHURCHILL ← Lower Ellick Wood — B3134
Track
Lower Ellick Farm
TO BLAGDON
Ellick House
B3134

WEST TWIN BROOK
EAST TWIN BROOK ←

Bracken ceases

BLACK DOWN

325m (1068ft)
OSBM
S1516

Beacon Batch Tumuli

60

BLACK DOWN

Grid Ref. OS 182 (1:50 000) 490 580   Approx. 1¾ miles

Climb to the highest spot on Mendip and look for miles over rolling hills and silvery sea. Black Down's acid moorland can be wet and will act like a sponge if it has rained recently so wellies may be advisable. High points are often windy so wrap up well if it is cold or wet for this hilly walk of almost two miles.

At the top of Burrington Combe on the left is a large parking area and almost opposite, on the right and higher up the hill, is a lay-by with a track leading off it past Ellick House. Follow this track with the house and its red post-box on the right and walk up into the hills.

Here and there the surface of the track itself is hard grey limestone, the very bones of the hill which have been swept clean by running water and passing feet. It is smooth and water-worn as the rain, which collects carbon dioxide whilst falling, is sufficiently acid to dissolve the rock.

Beside the track are blackthorn bushes. These are unmistakable for, as their name suggests, they have black bark and thorns often very long and sharp which, if you are unlucky enough to be pierced by one, seem to leave an irritant inside your skin to cause soreness for some time after the encounter. Their fine creamy-white flowers can be seen in early April and, in cold springs, arrive before the leaves appear giving a beautiful contrast of a dark bush with white blossom. The fruit in autumn is well known to makers of sloe gin as the blackthorn is the source of the sloe fruit. Sloes are dark blue in colour, with a white bloom, and taste extremely bitter. The initial nibble is not nasty but suddenly the berry then seems actually to dry up the mouth.

The trees growing on either side are ash and can be identified by their light-grey bark, especially on the branches, and in winter by their dark-grey buds. The leaves are compound and have a single stalk with individual saw-edged leaves growing in opposite pairs along its length. The flowers consist of frothy bunches of stems terminating in purple-brown tips which grow in clumps from its twigs before the leaves appear on the tree. Indeed ash, like oak, is almost the last tree to come into leaf and features in an old country rhyme which supposedly foretells the coming summer's rainfall:

If oak comes out before the ash
We will only have a splash.
If ash comes out before the oak
We will surely have a soak!

Ash flowers and leaves

The ash is a good indicator of limestone

Ash fruits are called keys and are winged seeds which form in bunches and spiral away on the breeze when ripe. Ash is a very typical tree of limestone country as it likes alkaline or base rich soils. It is common on Mendip, especially in Burrington Combe and the Cheddar and Ebbor Gorges and in other limestone areas such as parts of the Peak District National Park.

'White' butterflies may be seen on this limestone grassland although not all will belong to the 'white' family for some, strangely enough, will probably be members of the 'browns'. The large white is often here – a creamy-white butterfly with black tips to the leading edges of the forewings and it is the 'cabbage white' of gardens. Here it will choose the wild members of the cabbage family such as hedge mustard on which to lay its eggs.

The marbled white, which is about the same size as the large white but with pretty dappled-white markings, is in fact a 'brown'. Its larvae (caterpillars) feed on grass and the female lays her eggs in a most haphazard fashion: she merely scatters them among the grass stems as she flies.

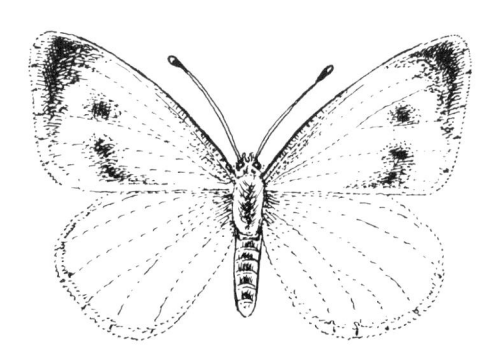

Large cabbage white (female).
A member of the 'white' family

Marbled white (male).
A member of the 'brown' family

At the top of the track where it comes out onto the hillside, the main route bears round to the right. Do not take this route but go straight on up the narrower path.

The whole of this northern hillside in front is dominated by a sheet of bracken. This ubiquitous fern may be seen in spring, unfurling its fronds from among last year's stems. If it comes out to early, frost will brown the soft new ends to the leaves. A little later on the landscape can be seen covered in a delightful light-green carpet; this will gradually darken as the year progresses and the plant grows taller; consequently, by high summer, the bracken will be above the shoulders of all but the tallest. In autumn bracken browns and dies back taking on a gingery-golden hue in low afternoon sunlight like the coat of an orang-utan. (See an illustration of bracken on page 114.)

Parts of the bracken are razor sharp and will cause fine deep cuts in unprotected hands and legs – so resist the temptation to pull at the leaves or stems or even to run through it.

MENDIP PROFILE

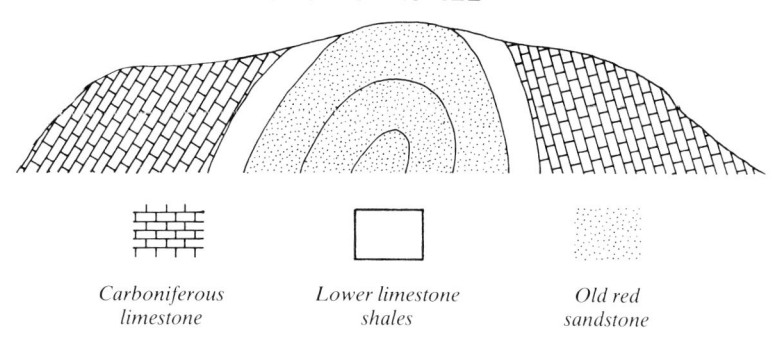

Carboniferous limestone   *Lower limestone shales*   *Old red sandstone*

At one time, in areas where few cereals were grown and straw was scarce, bracken was used for animal bedding even though, if eaten in quantity by stock, it is poisonous. Now, with improved transport systems to move straw from cereal areas and land improvement enabling more farmers to grow corn, this is no longer necessary. The bracken here owes its existence to frequent fires which sweep up from Burrington Combe from time to time. Its underground rhizomes protect it from flames and allow the plant to rise Phoenix-like from the ashes when all else is destroyed.

At about the point when the bracken is left behind, the underlying rock changes from limestone to sandstone. The ground will start to feel different underfoot. The rock itself is gritty and, as its name implies, like many tiny gravel grains all stuck together making it rough and coarse to the touch. Sandstone is impervious (water will not drain through it) and it does not crack and fissure as limestone does. The soil on the sandstone here is peaty, the vegetation not being broken down to the same extent as on limestone because of the lack of oxygen in these water-logged conditions.

The highest point on Mendip is now being approached and it is ironical that the apex of a range of hills well known for being limestone is, in fact, formed from sandstone. The truth of the matter is that the softer limestone has been dissolved and eroded away from the top of the fold or anticline to reveal the more hardwearing old red sandstone beneath. The sandstone outcrops at only three other places on Mendip, all of them high points. They are North Hill at Priddy, Beacon Hill close to Shepton Mallet and Pen Hill near Wells on which stands the very tall TV mast.

If it is not a time of drought, the path will be wetter than on the limestone and the plant-life changes quite suddenly. For the skilled botanist this change is enormous but even the untrained eye can spot some changes. The bracken ceases and this in itself is odd for the plant normally shuns limestone soils and seeks acid ones. As has been seen, fire has enabled bracken to spread on the limestone and the same fire has been extinguished by the wet nature of the acid sandstone soil thus preventing further spread of the bracken. It is replaced by low-growing woody plants like whortleberry, heather, gorse and purple moor grass.

Whortleberry (blaeberry or bilberry). Very tasty in pies

Whortleberry has a number of other names including bilberry and blaeberry and its fruit is much favoured by Americans. The leaves and stems of this plant turn a beautiful red in autumn but by then the small sweet black berries, which are ripe in July will probably have already disappeared.

There are three types of heather here: bell heather and common heather (ling) – the former having bigger and redder flowers – and cross leaved heath which can be identified by the arrangement of its leaves around the stem in whorls of four.

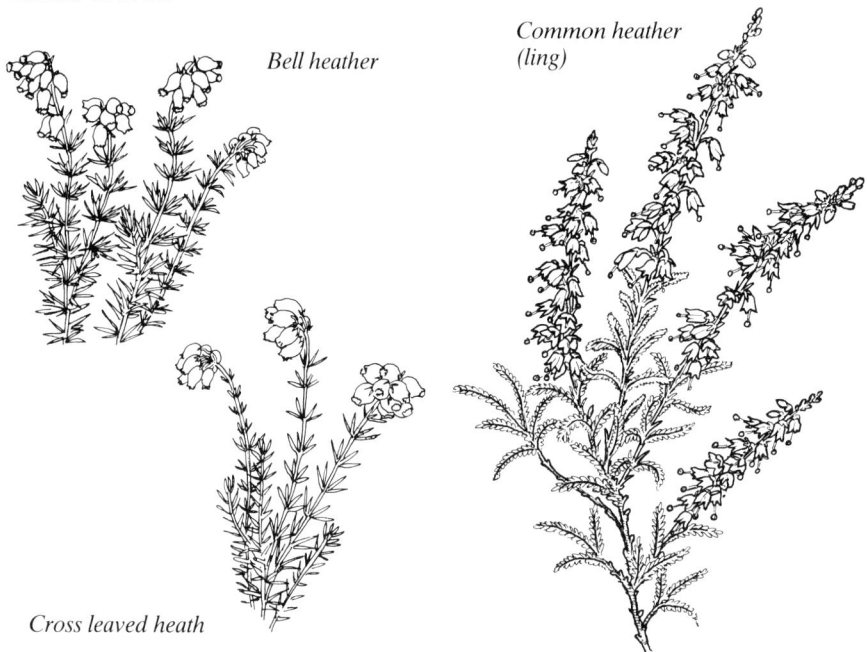

Bell heather

Common heather (ling)

Cross leaved heath

Looking back near the top of the slope on a clear day, the sparkling waters of Blagdon and Chew Valley lakes can be seen and, in the distance, the Black Mountains and the Brecon Beacons on the far side of the Channel.

At the strong wide cross track, turn right towards the triangulation point.

In summer especially, there should be a variety of birds here; listen first for skylarks singing high in the sky. The lark may be spotted hovering against the brightness or perhaps parachuting down on half-closed wings to land in the grass and disappear from view. A speckle-breasted meadow pipit may be making its high-voiced call from vegetation around about and perhaps the sound of someone apparently knocking two pebbles together may be heard. This is really the contact call of the stonechat – a bird a little smaller than a robin. The male stonechat has a black head, white collar and chestnut breast. Look out too for a very smart bird on the path or a nearby mound. When approached it will fly off a little way showing a white patch on the converts above its tail, revealing itself as a wheatear. Unlike the previous three birds, this is a summer migrant, wintering in warmer climates and only coming to Britain to breed before leaving again in autumn.

Wheatears
One of the earlier summer migrants to arrive

Female

Male

Stonechats
Their call is like the clicking together of stones

Male

Female

It may probably be noticed that there is no shortage of mounds for wheatears to use around here. Some of them, the round ones, are Bronze-Age tumuli and make up a collection called Beacon Batch. These round barrows (burial mounds) are remnants of the early Bronze Age dating from 1700 to 1200 BC, and other groups are to be found on North Hill and Beacon Hill, both high points mentioned already.

> *Not to be confused with the round barrows are a large number of other mounds dating back only as far as World War II. They were constructed here as a decoy town to attract enemy bombers.*

Continue onwards to the triangulation point OSBM S1516.

This concrete marker stands at 1,068 feet which, it may be considered, makes Black Down a mountain if 1,000 feet is taken as the height at which hills end and mountains begin. Although it can be very cold and bleak here in bad weather, it is hardly worthy of the name, especially when surrounded by the lush emerald-green fields of grass growing on limestone.

The views are superb on a clear day. From Pen Hill, with its extremely tall mast to the south-east, turn southwards to note the silver shapes of farm buildings in the middle-ground and the rocks of Cheddar Gorge beyond. In the distance, past the Poldens – a hogsback ridge of hills which runs from Street to Bridgwater – the Quantocks can be seen and, if it is really clear, Exmoor too. On the far side of Bridgwater Bay, standing on Somerset's north coast, are the large concrete boxes of the Hinkley Point nuclear power stations.

Down in the valley, the rim of Cheddar reservoir should be visible. To the north of the reservoir the top of the bare rockface of Callow Quarry is just visible standing at the end of the long straight track. To the right of this are the trees of Rowberrow Warren.

Rowberrow Warren is a plantation of mostly conifers although there is a proportion of beech trees for amenity and firebreak purposes. The conifer species are sitka and Norway spruce (the latter being the traditional Christmas tree), Scots and Coriscan pine and larch. Sitka spruce and Corsican pine are planted particularly for their rapid growth and the former, which hails from Alaska, produces more timber in a shorter time than any other tree. Except for the beech, all the above species are softwoods and have been introduced into Britain for commercial purposes.

Although it appears dense from a distance, the plantation is thinned from time to time to remove smaller trees which are used for fencing or pulp thus allowing the best specimens to grow more freely.

Almost due west above the plantation is Brean Down with Steep Holm and Flat Holm (with its lighthouse) situated beyond. Turning north past Weston-super-Mare there is a further area of woodland beyond Wrington and the swathe cut by a pylon line is clearly visible passing over the skyline.

Walk away from the triangulation point, with the numbers side directly behind, along the more defined of the two paths. At the major cross-paths turn right.

Look on the left here for the start of a small stream valley – the eastern-most course of a pair of streams known as East Twin Brook and West Twin Brook. They run down to a whole series of medium-sized caves for which the Burrington area is famous. East Twin terminates at East Twin Swallet or Swallow Hole – so called because the earth appears to swallow the water. Swallets are

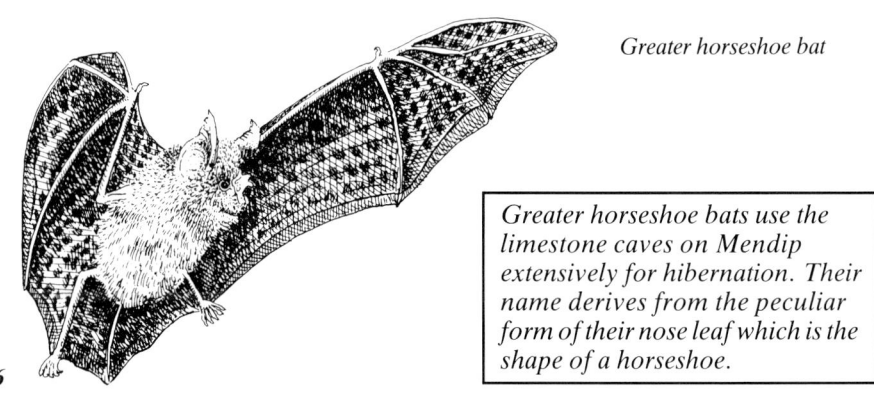

Greater horseshoe bat

Greater horseshoe bats use the limestone caves on Mendip extensively for hibernation. Their name derives from the peculiar form of their nose leaf which is the shape of a horseshoe.

apparent in many parts of Mendip. Some are like funnels with caves leading on from the bottom of the deep depression like that of Rod's Pot, while in others the cave entrance is choked and water simply filters through the rocks into underground passages. Choked swallets are sometimes excavated by enthusiastic pot-holers intent on discovering new caves like that of Sidcot Swallet which was 'dug' by members of the Sidcot School Speleological Society in 1925. On other occasions, usually after prolonged heavy rain or storms, the choke is cleared by the pressure of water and a new cave reveals itself to the eager explorer. One such is Grebe Swallet in Velvet Bottom which was first opened up by a flood in July 1968.

In the drier and sunnier areas of the hillside an adder (viper) may be encountered. It is one of the two common species of snakes in Britain. The adder prefers to inhabit dry heathland areas where it can bask in the sun and hunt the small mammals upon which it preys. The nature of its food means that the snake has to be poisonous, for it would be very difficult to capture and kill lively prey such as shrews and mice without this weapon. The snake stalks its quarry, bites it to inject venom, and then withdraws to avoid being bitten itself until the animal succumbs. The meal is then swallowed whole, relying upon its powerful digestive juices to break down the prey.

The adder is easy to recognise despite its base colour varying from light to dark green through to an almost chestnut red. It has a distinctive heavily-marked dark zig-zag line along its back, and on the head there is a 'V' or an inverted 'A' mark from which it is said to take its name. It is shorter and stockier than a grass snake and tends to avoid water which the grass snake enjoys. The pupils of its eyes are slit vertically to form a diamond shape unlike the round eye of the grass snake.

> *More people have died from insect stings in the last 90 years than from adder bites.*

The adder is viviparous (i.e. it produces live young as opposed to the grass snake which lays eggs) and does not have to rely on the heat of the sun for incubation, thus enabling the species to spread further north, as far as the top of Scotland in fact.

Whilst the adder is poisonous, it frightens easily and will hurry away if disturbed. People who get bitten have almost always interfered with the snake in some way and it will have bitten in self-defence. It is much better to leave the reptile alone to depart of its own accord for it will certainly not go out of its way to bite people.

Adder (viper)

*Although poisonous,
it is harmless if left alone*

In summer months there may be house martins and swallows hawking for insects over the bracken. House martins are stubbier than swallows with a similar but much shorter forked tail. In flight their distinctive white rump and white underparts show up against their black wings and apparently black bodies – their heads and backs are actually dark blue. The upperparts of the swallow are more noticeably dark blue, whilst their underparts are quite pink and their chins and foreheads a reddish chestnut. These birds are members of the same family – both being insect eaters which they catch in flight, and both living in close association with man. Martins hang their mud nests under the eaves of buildings, while swallows stand theirs on a beam or ledge in an outbuilding or garage. Swallows and martins arrive from Africa in spring and return there in autumn, gathering on telegraph wires beforehand in noisy groups almost as if discussing their travel plans.

The farm in the valley below, near Ellick House, keeps a herd of Guernsey cows – quite a rarity in a dairy county with a heavy majority of black and white Friesian herds. These cows, which give creamier milk than Friesians, are brown with white bellies and often have white patches on their legs. Quite a few may well be seen in the fields nearby.

On the left of the path here, is a single tree, the highest on the hill. It is a rowan (mountain ash) and has leaves remarkably like those of ash even though they do not belong to the same family. The rowan, which does well in acid soils, has white blossoms about May which precede the scarlet berries of early September. Although too sour for man's palate, they seem highly desirable to birds and quickly disappear in early autumn. The tree had a particular significance to crofters in Scotland and was planted close to the house to protect the holding against witchcraft.

Rowan branch with flowers and leaves.

Its berries are one of the earliest autumn fruits to appear

Descending the hill, the limestone will be regained. A path near the hedge bordering agricultural land will be reached. Follow this with the hedge to the left. Turn left at the track and back down the hill to the road.

SAND POINT

This wooden ladder stile has been built by the National Trust to allow easy access across this stone wall, thus saving it from unnecessary damage

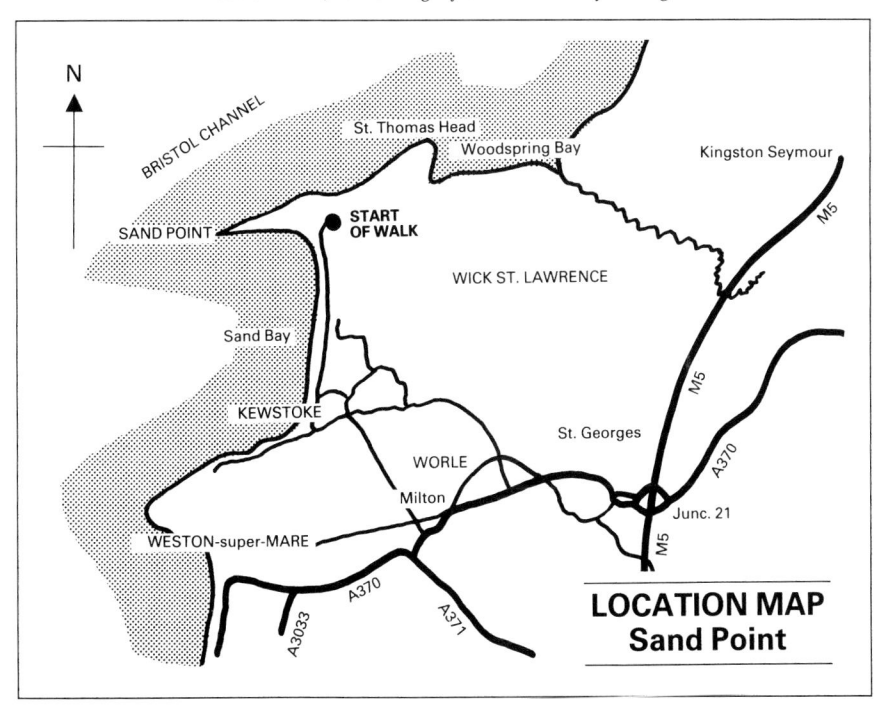

**LOCATION MAP
Sand Point**

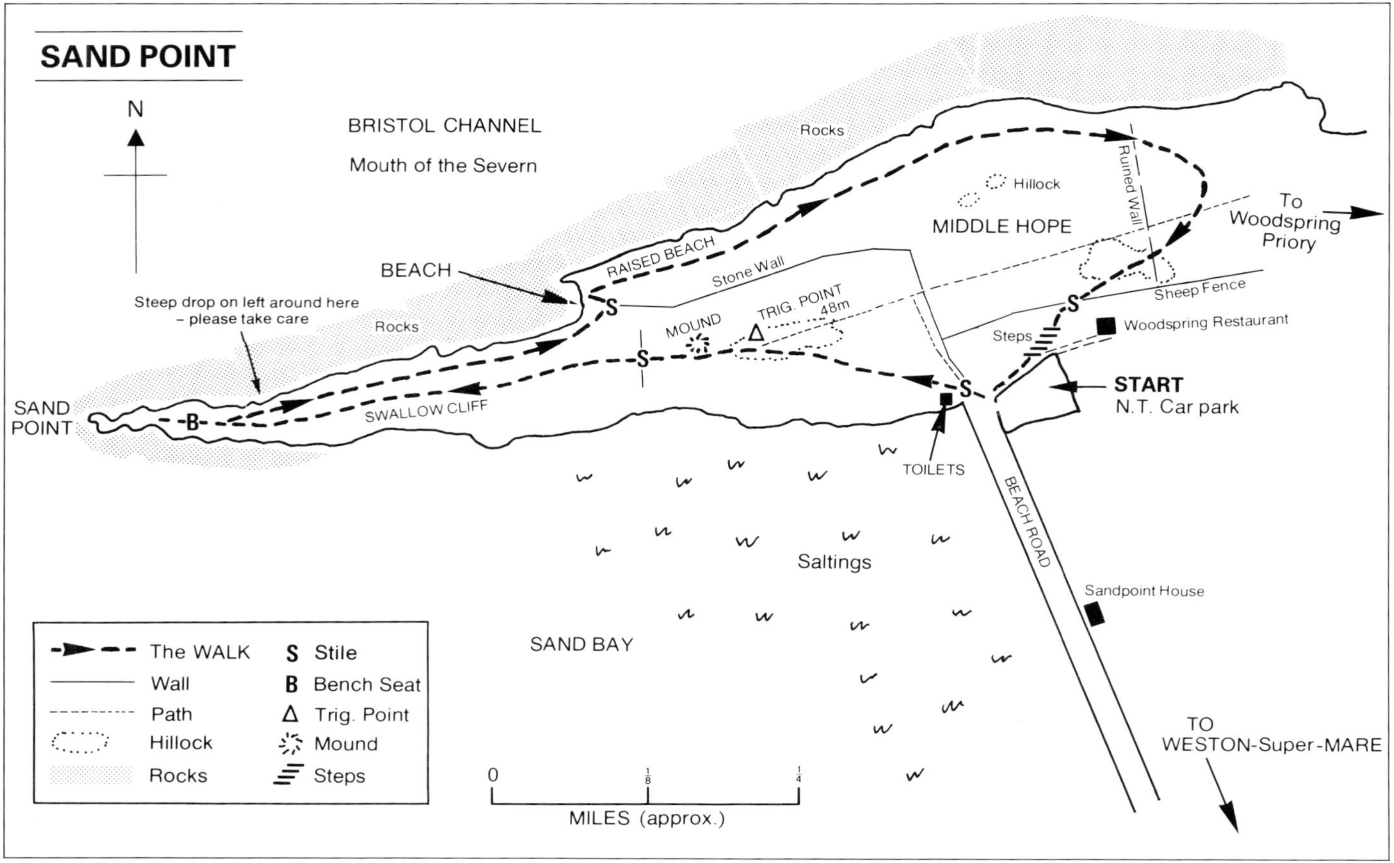
SAND POINT
N
BRISTOL CHANNEL
Mouth of the Severn
Rocks
Hillock
MIDDLE HOPE
Ruined Wall
To Woodspring Priory
BEACH
RAISED BEACH
Stone Wall
Steep drop on left around here – please take care
Rocks
S
MOUND
TRIG. POINT 48m
Sheep Fence
S
Woodspring Restaurant
Steps
S
START
N.T. Car park
SAND POINT
B
SWALLOW CLIFF
TOILETS
BEACH ROAD
Saltings
Sandpoint House
SAND BAY
TO WESTON-Super-MARE
The WALK
Wall
Path
Hillock
Rocks
S Stile
B Bench Seat
Trig. Point
Mound
Steps
0
1/8
1/4
MILES (approx.)

SAND POINT

Grid Ref. OS 182 (1:50 000) 330 659 Approx. 2½ miles

This walk will take you to the end of the northernmost of three finger-like promontories – Brean Down, Worlebury Hill and Sand Point – which project into the Bristol Channel. Being limestone, the walk should be fairly dry underfoot although, as it is exposed and can be very windy, a warm windproof jacket may be needed. The walk is about 2½ miles long and is quite steep in parts.

After leaving the National Trust car park, cross the lane and climb the stile to the right. Mount the steps and bear left where the path forks on either side of the wall.

Old man's beard grows over the bushes on the left of the path. It takes its name from its fluffy silvery seed-heads whose windborne seeds are scattered when they ripen in autumn. In woodland this plant grows strongly, climbing quite tall trees towards the light and old stems often hang down like the lianas that Tarzan swings on – although old man's beard is generally not strong enough for such gymnastics. It is a good indicator of limestone, the hard light-grey rock from which Sand Point is formed.

Old man's beard seed-head

The view from this side of the point is very fine with Weston Woods clothing the north side of Worlebury Hill, Birnbeck Pier jutting from Anchor Head at its westernmost point and the two islands of Steep Holm and Flat Holm standing out of the waters of the Bristol Channel. Further along the coast is Brean Down and in the distance the north coast of Somerset.

Nearer at hand, the green area at the bottom of the cliffs is a small section of saltmarsh on which glasswort grows. It is a succulent-like plant with fleshy stems and leaves which vary in colour from green to red. Glasswort is grazed readily by domestic animals and is said to be the major dietary item of the white horses and black bulls of the extensive saltmarshes in the Camargue in the south of France. Farmers tend to like saltmarsh grazing, especially for sheep, as an occasional flooding by salt water kills the parasites which lurk in frequently-used pastures. This small area is not large enough for grazing but is used by wading birds which spread onto the large expanse of mud flats exposed when the tide is out.

The path leads out onto a clearing carpeted with short grass and surmounted by a concrete triangulation point (OSBM 3269).

The fine turf here is grazed mainly by rabbits – a mammal popular in literature but unpopular in agriculture. Before myxomatosis spread so rapidly in the mid-fifties rabbits were extremely common, eating crops but also keeping areas of grassland like this clear of bushes, brambles and trees. Only 30 years ago there was far less undergrowth than today and pictures of places like Cheddar Gorge taken at that time clearly show this. It is on these stretches of short turf that many of our limestone flowers grow so well. Constant cutting back of the bushes and scrub is the only way to conserve such plants and nowadays the teeth of rabbits are replaced by the sickles and saws of conservation volunteers.

Green food presents the plant-eaters (herbivores) with something of a problem for, unless they can break down the cellulose parts of the plant, the food they eat is almost valueless. Cows get over this by having four stomachs, swallowing their food as they graze and later bringing it up in balls of cud to chew at leisure. Rabbits approach the problem differently. Part of the lower half of their gut (caecum) is a dead-end terminating in the appendix. This contains large quantities of bacteria which feed on the green plants which the rabbit eats. As digestion continues, some of these bacteria are swept out and are eventually excreted in soft membrane-covered pellets. At certain times of the day, the rabbit produces these droppings which are different from the fairly-hard brown fibrous balls often seen in small heaps outside their holes. The soft pellets are loaded with bacteria from the caecum and are thus very rich in protein. The rabbit immediately eats them. This activity is called coprophagy and is necessary because the food value of the soft pellets has to be absorbed by the upper part of the rabbit's digestive system although it only becomes available in the lower half.

> *A doe rabbit can, theoretically, mother or grandmother over 40 young in any year. The doe has no 'season' and conception is stimulated by the act of mating. Although born blind and naked a young rabbit reaches sexual maturity within 12 weeks.*

Cross the green and follow the path via the stile to the point.

Three plants are worth looking out for here and I have particularly chosen coastal species. The rounded pink flowerheads of thrift may be seen from April to mid-summer growing on stems from its green cushion of leaves and, even in October, I have spotted the pale skeletons of flowerheads still on the plant. It was once pictured on the old twelve-sided threepenny piece because of its name. Rock samphire grows here too. It has light-green fleshy leaves which, like those of glasswort, are a frequent feature of plants which have to survive in a salty atmosphere and pale-yellow flowers appearing between July and autumn. It is a member of the carrot family and, although its roots are not eaten, the leaves and stems were once cooked and consumed like asparagus.

Pink thrift grows from a cushion of vivid-green leaves

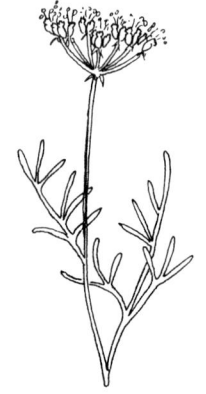

Light-green fleshy leaves and pale-yellow flowers are the hallmarks of rock samphire

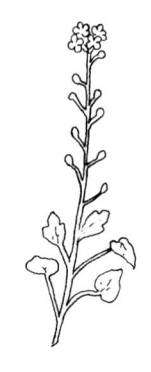

Scurvy grass with its rounded leaves often grows in gaps in rocks

The third plant is also edible and its rounded green leaves can often be observed in gaps in the rocks. This is scurvy grass – it is not a grass despite its name – which has been eaten in the past by sailors who found it very effective in combating scurvy.

The sloping rocks on the south side are clearly coloured in bands, the topmost being yellow before changing to a strip of black above the seaweed growth. This does not result from natural colouring or tar stains but derives from a covering of lichen. The yellow variety is *caloplaca thallincola* which commonly grows above the high-water mark and the black one is *verrucaria maura* which is abundant at the high-water mark.

It is surprising how many outside surfaces support lichens and there are few exposed rocks where much of the stone itself can actually be seen. Several species may be encountered during these walks especially on branches of bushes and on stone walls. Lichens are very good monitors of pollution; they are practically absent in some industrial areas and yet grow luxuriantly in the remote rural parts of Scotland. I find the biggest difficulty with lichens is their names for they do not often have common English ones. There is a book mentioned in the bibliography if more information is required about lichens.

> *Lichens are a fascinating mixture of a fungus and an alga. They pair up to form a symbiotic relationship – each benefiting from the partnership and only surviving because of it.*

Return past the bench-seat and bear to the left along the cliff-top path but take care as the path is quite narrow with a steep drop on the left.

One of my favourite maritime plants grows on the cliff-edge here and its white flowers with blushing pink-tinged sepal tube are around from May until September although the dried sepal tube can be seen after this. It is sea campion, a relative of bladder campion. Not only will it tolerate a salty atmosphere, it is also prepared to grow in the polluted soil of waste heaps which are found around old lead mines. Those near Priddy are a fine example.

Follow the path to the wall and climb over the stile.

The grassy area found here is a raised beach. This was a beach before the last ice-age when the sea-level was about 16 feet (5 metres) higher than at present – the subsequent glacial period causing the sea-level to fall. The raised beach gradually soiled over and now supports grass rather than seaweed.

Climb down onto the seashore on the left.

On first reaching the beach the rock, on the left, can be clearly seen in layers. The grey rock is limestone and was formed under a warm shallow sea where large quantities of shellfish were present. As these animals died their hard outside cases fell to the sea-bed and slowly built up there among the silts to form limestone.

As the rock was still being formed, a number of volcanic eruptions took place forcing molten lava out over the sea-bed where it cooled rapidly into rounded forms called 'pillows'. The lava, now a rock called olivine basalt, is only found towards the western end of the point but here can be seen layers of tuffs, a soft kind of volcanic fragmentary rock, which make the reddish-brown bands – in some parts veined white with calcite. Water-worn lumps on the beach can be picked up here and they remind me a little of faggots wrapped in caul fat.

SAND POINT SOIL/ROCK PROFILE

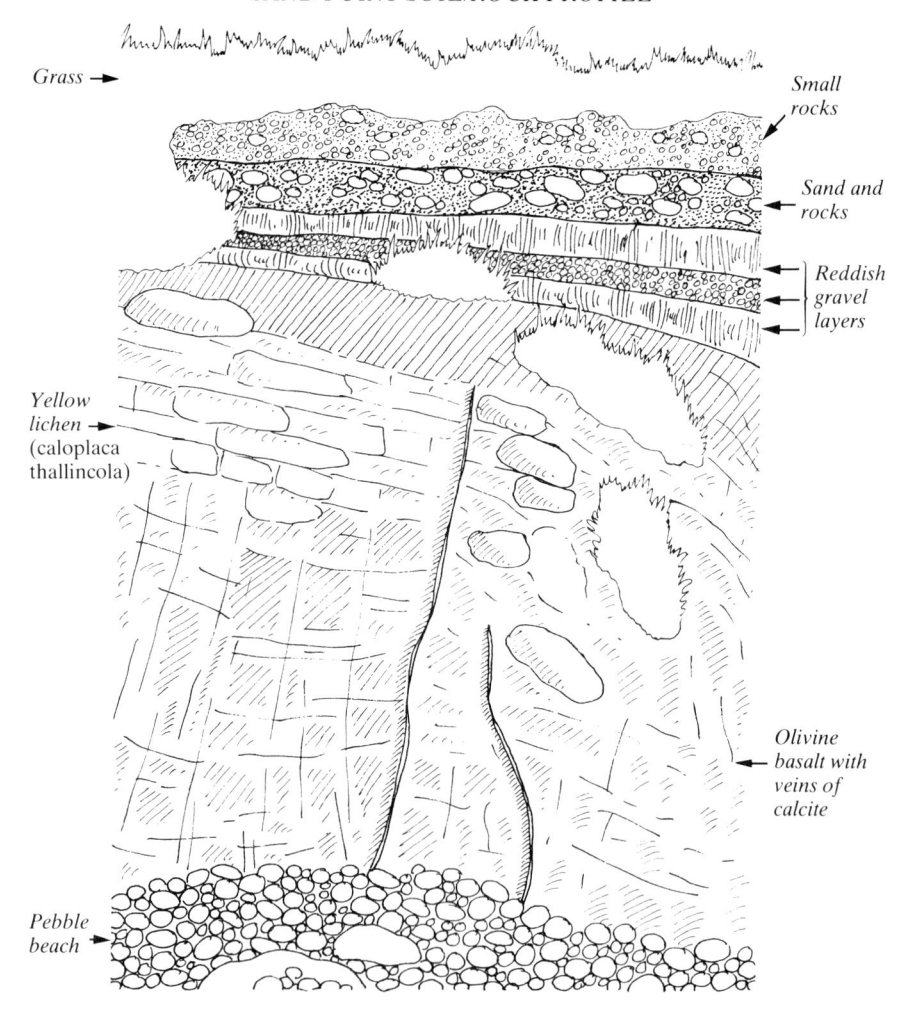

Grass →

Small rocks →

Sand and rocks →

Reddish gravel layers →

Yellow lichen → (caloplaca thallincola)

Olivine basalt with veins of calcite →

Pebble beach →

If the tide is out the rocks can be explored here but beware of the slippery seaweeds. These algae are often given scant attention but are worth looking at, especially as three types of wrack found here are easy to tell apart. Generally, the various species live in different belts (zones) down the shore as each requires differing lengths of time in water and in air. Strangely enough, the standard zoning is quite mixed up here and it is believed that this may be to do with the high tidal range or the quantity of sediments in the water of the Bristol Channel.

> *The Bristol Channel has an approximate rise and fall of 47 feet which makes it second only in the world to the St. Lawrence River in Canada.*

Flat wrack is without any air sacs and the end of each flat stem is divided and may be swollen. Egg wrack has single air sacs in the middle of each frond which has no midrib. Some of these bladders are very large and will pop when trodden on. Finally, there is bladder wrack itself with a midrib and neat bladders on either side, usually in pairs. Hidden in deep recesses under these seaweeds other interesting finds may be made. At the very least, by lifting back the fronds, some good fossils should be found such as small shellfish or even the spiral shape of an ammonite.

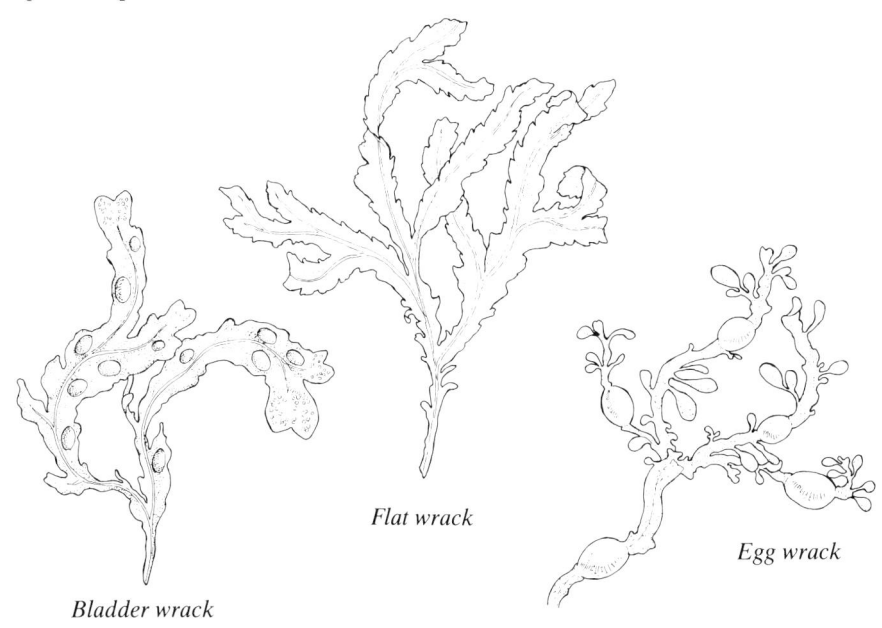

Flat wrack

Egg wrack

Bladder wrack

Hermit crabs are another favourite of mine. An apparently empty winkle or whelk shell inspected more closely may reveal a small crab's claw blocking the entrance. If the shell is put down and watched quietly, the occupant will eventually emerge and scuttle away with its borrowed home. As hermit crabs grow, their shell – being another creature's skeleton – does not grow with them. They have to look for a larger shell to protect their soft, fleshy and vulnerable tail and, in time, they will move up from a large winkle to a small whelk shell.

Hermit crab in a whelk shell.

Its right claw is larger and closes the entrance against enemies when the crab is inside

The dog whelk has only recently come to live this far up the Channel, previously being found only as far east as Blue Anchor near Minehead. Whelks are carnivores (meat-eaters) and the main prey of the dog whelk is the barnacle. Barnacles are small light-grey domed shells that often cover rocks so completely that there is hardly a space between them. They can crowd over 30,000 into a square yard and, not surprisingly, are the most common animal on rocky shores. They also cling to piers and even to the bottom of boats necessitating in hulls having to be scraped regularly. Although they look like shellfish, possibly smaller versions of the limpet, they are in fact relatives of shrimps and crabs. If a shell is inspected carefully it will be seen that it is not all in one piece but is constructed of a number of plates. The acorn barnacle, as it is properly known, is able to open a trapdoor at the top of its body and protrude a number of feathery appendages which are continually pushed out and pulled in, hopefully catching small marine prey on the way. British acorn barnacles have six plates surrounding the trapdoor. During the mid-forties, an Australian barnacle started to colonise the south coast, gradually spreading westwards around Land's End and back up towards Bristol. It can be distinguished from the British species by the fact that it has only four plates around the opening.

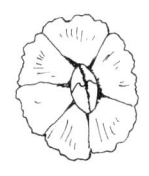

British acorn barnacle with 6 plates

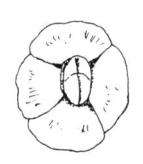

Australian acorn barnacle with 4 plates

Following the spread of the Australian version came the dog whelk for, as its food increased, so it was able to extend its range. Australian barnacles have now spread so prolifically that it is believed they may become the most common of the species around Britain. Whelks, unlike many carnivores, do not have to do much running about to catch their prey. Instead, they just crawl over to a patch of barnacles and force their feeding tube through the trapdoor of one, pour in digestive juices and suck out the contents to leave an empty shell. Indeed, such empty shells may be found, the four or six plates still in place but the trapdoor gone, stuck to the rocks on the shore. There are some varieties of sea shells illustrated on page 120.

Return to the shingle and climb back onto the raised beach, walking along between the shore and the stone wall.

On the far side of the stone wall is a large patch of elder bushes. These should not be confused with alders which are trees generally found near streams, as elders could never be called trees even though they may grow tall and stout. When young their stems are filled with a white pith and from these it is easy to make pea-shooters. It is this feature that gives the elder its name, a corruption of the Anglo-Saxon word for 'hollow tree'. As the bush ages, its stem develops into a hard white wood which at one time was carved into any instrument needing a point such as a comb or a fine pricker used by a watchmaker. Like the rowan, it has a great tradition in folklore and to burn elder wood on the fire is said to bring bad spirits into the house.

Elder is one of the first plants to push out new leaves in spring and is an early sign of warmer days to come. Although prompt with its leaves, elder flowers, in their great creamy-white clusters and with their heavy scent, do not appear until May or June. Some people make them into wine but I prefer elder-flower 'champagne' myself, because it is ready to drink quickly and it is refreshing on hot days.

Elderberries follow soon after the flowers and a good year will see bushes laden with a burden of fruit at the end of August and in September. Then they are especially favoured by starlings who gather in their branches in large clamorous flocks. The juicy fruits can be made into more wine or used to flavour pies and jellies.

Elder flowers, leaves and berries

An elder bush is often an indicator of a nearby badger sett as it likes to grow on disturbed ground; the soil around a sett is turned over at frequent intervals either from new digging or by the inhabitants searching for food. Rabbits, which sometimes share setts or live in the same area, do not like to eat the leaves and shoots and so they are allowed to sprout unmolested. As badgers eat the berries, whose seeds pass through the animal without damage, elders will sometimes grow from dung deposited near the sett.

Badgers make good use of the elder, particularly in clay areas, for they clean mud from their claws on its thick soft yellow-grey bark. Whether they do this because the elder happens to be handy or because the texture of its bark is suitable is difficult to say but it is common to find the trunks of bushes which grow near setts to be deeply scored by the long claws of a badger's forefoot.

At the end of the wall, the pasture runs from the raised beach and up the steep grassy hillside which has been terraced into horizontal paths by the passage of many sheep. Unless running in fear few domestic animals will go straight up or down a slope such as this but will either follow the contours or take a zig-zag course to avoid falling on the slippery turf.

Duck (left) and drake mallard in breeding plumage

Out at sea, mallards can often be spotted, sometimes in groups or 'rafts'. These are very common ducks and are probably the best known of all duck species because they turn up in parks with ponds and almost any kind of waterside area. They are the ducks that children 'go and feed'. For most of the year the drake (male) is brightly plumaged with a bottle-green head, chestnut breast, blue flashes on his wings and a curly tail. In late July and August though, mallards moult to renew their feathers and, like many water-birds, lose all their flight feathers at once. At this time, the male takes on the drab brown plumage of the female so as to escape detection by camouflage. They usually take up residence in saltmarshes like those on the south side of Sand Point.

In winter, groups of mallard will form into courtship assemblies and at the instigation of one bird the whole party will indulge in a courtship display. The drakes perform one part of the dance which is a complicated ritual involving a lot of splashing, whistling and quacking while the females incite them, each possibly choosing a particular mate which she tries to lead out of the group.

Whilst walking along the raised beach, a large round hillock appears on the right with a green track cutting the left-hand shoulder of the rise. Cross the ruined wall which, at its seaward end, can only be identified by bramble and elder bushes although more stones are visible on the hillside. Bear right and climb up the green track.

On a clear day the view up the Channel from here is superb. Clevedon nestles into the hills on the right with its pier jutting out to sea. In the distance the graceful outlines of the Severn Bridge can be seen spanning, in a single sweep of over a mile, the waters of the Bristol Channel. Inland of Clevedon, the M5 motorway runs down through a cleft in Tickenham Hill after leaving one of the most impressive pieces of highway engineering in Britain and descends to the low flat moors, barely climbing again until south of Bridgwater.

When the sheep fence can be seen running along to the right, turn sharp right parallel to the fence.

Woodspring Priory with its stone tower can be seen down on the left. The Priory was begun here in the 1220s in a chapel dedicated to St. Thomas Becket. It seems that the manor at 'Worspring' was owned by one of Becket's murderers and that his grandson founded the priory by way of penance. There was always a shortage of money and it took many years to build; the chancel and the Lady Chapel were not completed for a hundred years. Things looked up during the next century though, and a barn, church and hospital were built.

By this time Henry VIII was already in dispute with Rome but rather than argue with the king, the whole community (all eight of them) signed the document acknowledging Henry VIII as Supreme Head of the Church. Craftily, however, they had already disposed of most of the priory lands. The community was finally suppressed two years later in 1536.

The priory buildings were used mainly for agricultural purposes until the end of the last century when they became a golf club. At the end of World War I they were bought for conversion to a hotel but luckily nothing came of this scheme and the National Trust finally bought the estate in order to conserve it.

Unfortunately it is not possible to get to the priory from here – it is reached by going back to Weston-super-Mare and then returning on a road parallel to Sand Bay.

Go back across the old wall which is in a better state up here and walk towards Birnbeck Pier in the distance and thus to a stile in the sheep fence and descend the steps. At the bottom, turn right onto the lane, and return to the car park.

Where the track is left behind, a number of white poplars have been planted. These trees are commonly used as wind-breaks in sandy areas as they put out suckers from the roots and so rapidly establish a good number of plants to provide shelter. They have leaves with up to three lobes which are glossy dark-green on the upper surface and have a white matted underside, from which they take their name.

White poplar leaf

YATTON

The Little River is an ideal place for frogs and their predators – grass snakes

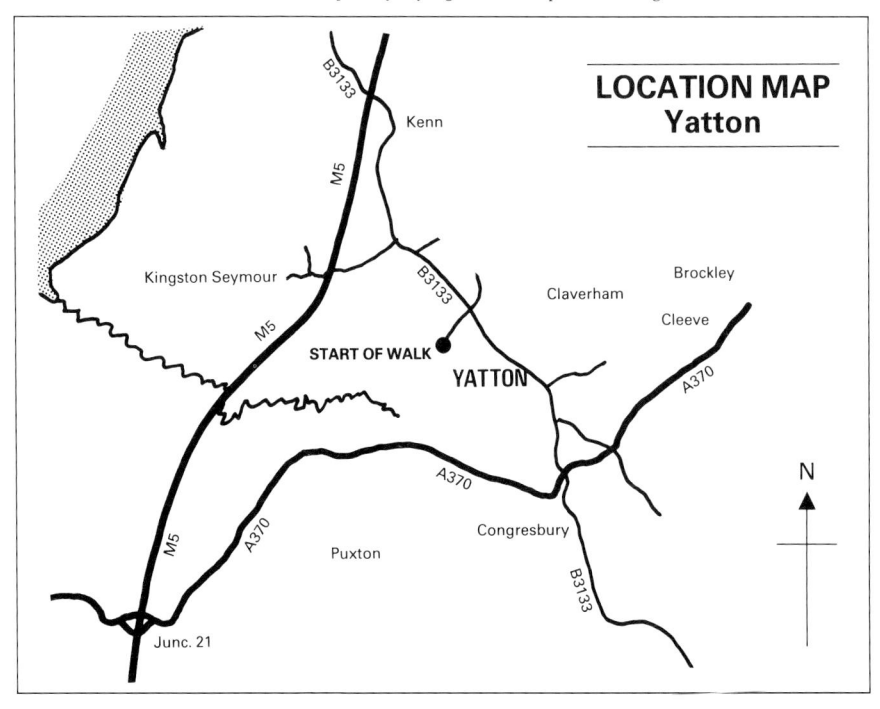

**LOCATION MAP
Yatton**

80

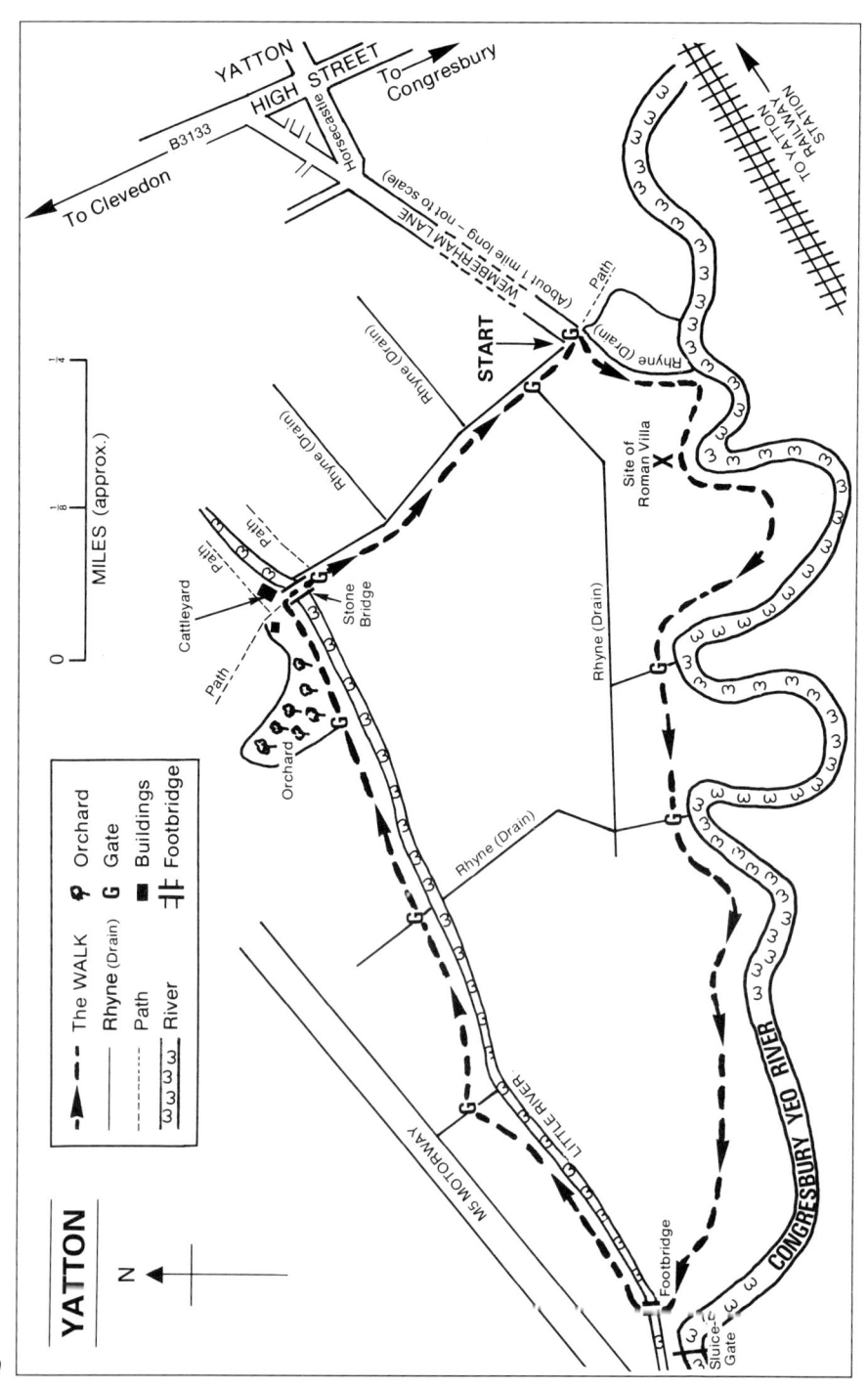

YATTON

Grid Ref. OS 182 (1:50 000) 408 654 **Approx. 2¼ miles**

This is a flat walk over pasture land with rivers and rhynes – it can be wet in winter. The route goes across fields beside the Congresbury Yeo River to the M5 motorway and then back across the levels. The valley here has been used for communications since Roman times and, as well as the river, a modern motorway and a mainline railway pass very close by.

If parking a vehicle, do not block any gateways. Pass through the two gates at the end of the road and, walking on top of the bank, keep to the right of the hedge which surrounds the final stretch of the Wemberham Lane rhyne.

This sort of thick hedgerow is perfect for small birds like the wren and the dunnock (hedge-sparrow). Whilst the former is our smallest very common bird, the goldcrest and the firecrest, which are smaller still, are not as rare as were once thought. Wrens are pert little birds with brown speckled plumage and an upright tail. They are extremely noisy, scolding their enemies in cross tones from hedgebottoms and singing their very loud song with great gusto; a song which can be identified by the whirring sound at the end like that of a clockwork motor running down. Male wrens build several nests in spring and their mates then choose the one they favour most. When hatched the young birds are reared sufficiently quickly for wrens for produce two broods in most years.

The maintenance of wren numbers in this way is important for, like all very small birds and mammals, they have a problem in keeping warm in winter because their body surface area is large in proportion to their volume. Many succumb during cold weather especially if there is prolonged snow and the wren's insect food is scarce.

> *In an attempt to keep warm in winter wrens will crowd together in roost sites. Up to 46 have been found in a single nest box.*

The dunnock is larger than the wren but more retiring in its habits spending most of its time searching through the leaf-litter for invertebrates. Although called the hedge-sparrow, it is not related in any way to the sparrows. They have the broad bills of seed-eaters whilst that of the dunnock has the slim beak of the insectivore. Its plumage provides excellent camouflage as its back feathers are mottled brown and black and those of its head, breast and underparts

The wren is a little bird with a loud song

The dunnock (hedge-sparrow) is a quiet secretive bird

are grey. Dunnocks and wrens are frequent garden visitors although, as birds that feed on or near the ground, they do not like to leave close cover. They rarely use bird-tables but, unusually, both species utilise the one in my garden.

Follow the bank to the river and turn right to cut off the bend and walk across to meet the river again.

Here, on the right, looking down from the rise made by the bank, the ground is rather rough and bumpy. This area is the site of a Roman villa. Although the Romans had occupied Britain in AD 43 this part of the country was not settled intensively until almost 250 years later. At that time Britain was in a state of some unrest and it is strange to find development on this scale under those circumstances. Some surmise that the occupiers were Romans displaced from France. In any event the villa, here at Wemberham, was a grand affair and one of the wealthiest in the area, which, being fertile, tended to have such agriculturally-based properties at fairly frequent intervals.

Wemberham Villa was discovered in 1884 when land drains were being laid. Twelve rooms were found, forming only part of the house; six were floored with mosaics, four of which were patterned. The building consisted of two storeys and had the benefit of underfloor heating. I suspect that water levels were lower then – possibly by up to two feet – for it seems likely, from adjacent discoveries, that corn was grown here. The nearby river, the Congresbury Yeo, was navigable past this point thus providing easy transport for heavy or bulky goods from the villa's private landing point. Woodspring Museum in Weston-super-Mare has displays about Wemberham and the Roman occupation of the area including parts of the original mosaic floors.

Follow the river for a short way and then bear off right along the flood bank to cut off the corner of the river.

At times field voles occupy this bank which must provide drier accommodation than its surroundings. These are timid little grey-brown mammals with blunt noses, furry ears and very short furred tails. Their holes may be seen in the ground, often with very short grass in the

Field vole

immediate vicinity which is known as a 'vole garden'. The vole, too scared sometimes to wander far for food, will pop out of the entrance, nip off a grass-stem or other vegetation and retreat out of danger and into its burrow to feed. Field voles are probably the most strictly vegetarian of all the common small mammals and form the base diet of many carnivores, especially foxes and birds of prey. It is therefore hardly surprising that, living in such an open location, they do not like to venture far from safety.

Pass through the gate – note the hawthorn on the right which has been rubbed smooth by cattle. The bank forks at this point; take the right fork to cut off the next river corner.

A lone heron may be seen here, either stalking with slow steps in the muddy edges of the river (look for its big tracks if the bird itself is not seen), standing motionless on the bank, or even perched on the sluice-gate machinery in the distance. Although it is hard to believe, these large ungainly birds quite often

> *Heron chicks, if they feel threatened, will, as a form of defence, lean over the edge of the nest and regurgitate the remains of their last fishy meal over intruders – including people!*

perch in trees and gather in a colony (heronry) to build their nests in the tops of a group of trees. Heronries will often have chicks in them as early as March.

The heron has a wide carnivorous diet which, apart from fish and eels, also includes frogs and small mammals. It catches its prey by slow stealthy patient movements and a lightning devastating grab with its long dagger-like bill. Like many water birds, it often hunts at night and more than once I have been alarmed on a quiet moonlit walk by the sudden wingflaps of a departing heron. In spite of its high-nesting habit, the heron's flight always appears heavy and laboured and often it comes under attack, especially from crows and rooks. When this happens, it flys lower and lower until it almost touches the ground, often protesting with harsh cries of 'Fraa-ank fraa-ank'.

Heron

A variety of plants may be found growing on the dredgings from the river which are thrown up onto the bank. In particular, thistles seem to thrive on this silty soil and in autumn their fluffy seed-heads will attract goldfinches.

Goldfinch on thistle

A flock of goldfinches is called a 'charm'

Continue along the path through another gate almost as far as the sluice-gate, turn sharp right and carefully cross the footbridge, turn right and follow the field boundary by the river to the gate. Pass through the gate and turn right to follow the field boundary once again.

The river is tidal as far as the sluice-gate and the occasional seashore bird may been seen here as a result. As the route is followed beside the Little River, the adjacent motorway is the M5. In an age of agricultural intensification and continuing destruction of wildlife habitats, motorway verges have provided small areas of respite for some species. Most people, when travelling along such roads, will have noticed a kestrel (windhover) maintaining station with its rapidly fluttering wings and broad tail as it searches the ground beneath for suitable prey. Kestrels will feed on beetles although they prefer mice or voles if they can find them. It seems to be a common fallacy that predators in general take items of prey much bigger than, in fact, they do. Thus foxes eat many voles and mice while a kestrel would find a rabbit impossible deal with. I once watched a kestrel trying to fly off with a baby rabbit which had hardly grown its fur. Eventually the bird had to give up the unequal struggle for it was just not capable of carrying the weight. The rough and largely unmown motorway verges harbour many small mammals ensuring that their numbers remain fairly high thus attracting kestrels.

In addition to field voles, the verges are likely to provide a habitat for both common and pygmy shrews. These tiny insectivorous mammals with long quivering noses and tiny black eyes rush hither and thither in a constant search for food. Like the wrens they suffer badly from heat loss and, to maintain their high metabolic rate and hence their body temperature, they have to eat something close to their own weight in invertebrate prey every day. Shrews are very quarrelsome creatures and, when fighting amongst themselves, give high-pitched chirrupy, insect-like cries. These are audible to humans up to a certain age but become too high for older ears to hear. Other small mammals tend to avoid shrews; it is claimed that they possess a toxic saliva which can be fatal to animals as small as mice. They rely a great deal on scent both to find their way around and to locate their prey, and they have scent glands with which to mark their territories. These scent glands make shrews distasteful to animals such as

Kestrel

Common shrew    *Woodmouse*

cats which will kill them but then abandon the corpses uneaten. Only owls are known to eat shrews with any regularity.

Where there is woodland adjacent to a motorway or the trees planted on the embankments are growing well, woodmice and bank voles are likely to be found. The bank vole is more gingery than the field vole and tends to like woodland; it climbs well and is fond of nuts and fruit. Woodmice – or 'fieldmice' as they are sometimes known – are small and brown with very long tails and with white underparts and a faint buff line running between their front legs. They too, like to climb and will make winter stores of nuts or berries in old birds' nests or nest-boxes.

While motorway and roadside verges have provided very suitable habitats for all of these small mammals, they do have their disadvantages – a major one being discarded bottles and tins. All of these animals like to explore new holes and little entrances and empty bottles are prime candidates. The animal wriggles in through the neck and slides down inside only to find that it cannot climb back up the slippery glass and escape. Eventually it dies of starvation, or cold if there happens to be water at the bottom, and its body decomposes until only a few bones remain. I understand that the record for the number of skulls in a single bottle is 27; I once found 19 and, on many occasions, between six and ten skulls, so this is by no means an unusual occurrence.

> *Figures published a few years ago indicated that 9 million small mammals perish each year in 11 million or so discarded bottles and cans.*

The Little River on the right with its damp banks is an ideal habitat for frogs and for grass snakes too. Frogs are amphibians which means they can live both on land and in the water. On land, they move about by leaping and trust to speed to escape danger. In water their powerful legs and large webbed feet will help them make a rapid getaway and they can remain hidden underwater with only their eyes and nostrils showing above the surface. Frogs have many predators so it is fortunate that they breed so prolifically, returning to the pond of their birth in February or March where each female lays up to 3,000 eggs before the adults disperse.

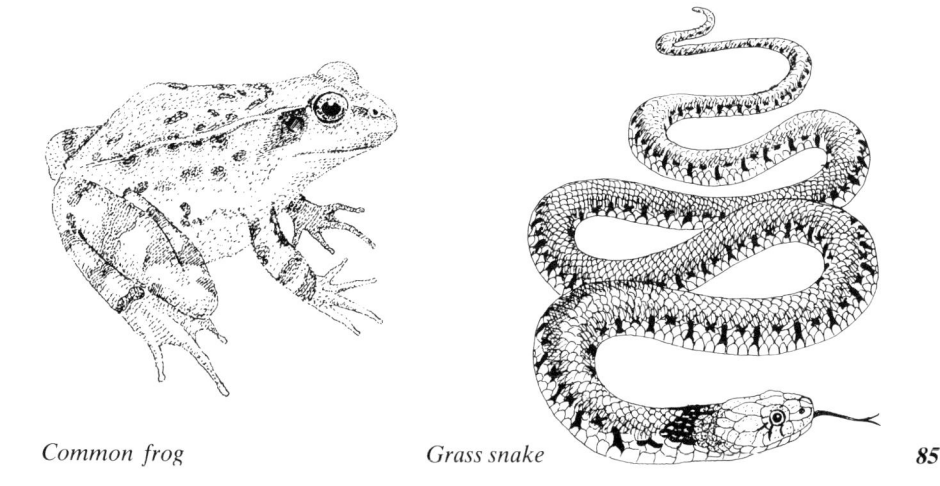

Common frog   *Grass snake*

Frogs feed on insects (sometimes catching them with flicks of their long sticky tongues), slugs, snails and worms. In autumn, when such prey becomes scarce, frogs go into hibernation, diving to the bottom of a pond or ditch and burying themselves in the mud. Although they breathe through their nostrils on land, when submerged all winter, they breathe through their skin which enables them to take in sufficient oxygen to survive in their torpid state.

One of the major predators of the frog is the grass snake. This reptile, which is harmless to humans, can be seen basking in the spring sunshine after its emergence from hibernation. Being cold-blooded animals they rely on the heat of the sun to warm their bodies and help the blood course round so that they have the energy to hunt. When basking they flatten their bodies as much as possible in order to obtain the maximum benefit from this heat source. Grass snakes are olive-green in colour with black markings along their flanks; much the most noticeable identification mark is their yellow collar behind the head. The pupils of their eyes are round (the adder has vertical slits) and they grow up to three feet long.

Grass snakes, if unable to avoid capture, will feign death or exude a foul-smelling fluid which they tend to spray about when picked up. They eat frogs and newts, toads and fish and occasionaly small mammals. The aquatic creatures are often caught in the water for the grass snake swims readily and is known in some places as the 'water snake'. The female lays soft-shelled eggs during the summer months in a manure heap or rotting vegetation, relying on the temperature of the immediate environment and the sun to incubate them, which can take up to ten weeks. It is this need for warmth for breeding that controls the distribution of the grass snake and it is rarely found north of the Scottish border.

Pass through the gate and keep to the bank of the Little River.

The path goes through a gate into a cider orchard. Sadly, for one of the area's well-known traditions, such orchards are becoming scarce as cider-making at the farm is a drying art. Such orchards are generally found near the farmsteading and are grubbed out to free additional land close to the farm, although this orchard, whilst it is near farm buildings, has no farmhouse nearby.

A squirrel may be seen here for, apart from humans, they are the only wholly-diurnal (daytime active) British mammal. In autumn these animals enjoy the bounty of the orchard too. They are grey squirrels, rodents which came to this country from America. They tend to be more positively grey in winter, for their coats are often flecked and streaked with gingery-brown in the summer months to such an extent that casual observers are sometimes fooled into thinking they have seen a red squirrel. Squirrels do not hibernate but they may spend several days in their nest (drey) if the weather is especially bad. It is quite usual, however, to see the foraging signs of squirrels, or even the animals themselves, out in the snow on sunny days.

A squirrel's drey looks a little like a magpie's nest but normally the twigs from which it is constructed still have their leaves attached. This leafy ball is located in a fork of the tree, probably against the trunk, and is lined with grass, moss and leaves. Alternatively, the animals may make use of a suitable hollow in a branch or trunk, and here they will breed. Female grey squirrels can have two litters in a year, one in early spring and the other in summer. The young are born blind, naked and deaf and take up to seven weeks to leave the nest.

*Grey squirrel and winter drey
lined with grass and shredded bark*

Grey squirrels cache nuts and acorns in autumn against the winter but often forget their hiding places, thus unwittingly planting future trees. This, in some part, makes up for the damage they cause by bark-stripping.

At first they have long thin tails and look distinctly rat-like; in fact foresters, who dislike squirrels, call them 'tree-rats'. Their bad reputation derives from their habit of stripping bark from trees. While red squirrels live in coniferous woodlands, the grey ones prefer deciduous hardwoods and cause considerable damage by bark stripping.

The scarring is bad enough and can lead to attack by disease; but worse still, the squirrel may strip the bark all round the trunk, killing the tree whch may have been nurtured for 30 or 40 years. This naturally frustrates the forester.

Look for a drey in the row of trees next to the stream. Most of them are horse chestnuts and can be recognised either by their leaves in 'hands' of five or seven, by their fruit (conkers) or by the scars on the twigs. These are reminiscent of horseshoe prints – complete with nail marks – and give the tree its name. The horse-chestnut is one of the first trees to change colour and lose its leaves in autumn. In spring the new leaves appear beautifully delicate as they break out of the well-known sticky buds, soon to be followed by white flowers which stand upright in bunches like candles on a Christmas tree. (See illustrations on page 115).

Walk up to the buildings and turn right over the old stone bridge and through a gate. Note the unusual cattle-yard on the left with the whole of one side sloping down to the river. Follow the rhyne, keeping it to the left. (Do not cross the metal bridge.)

Look out for the land drains which spill into this rhyne draining the pasture on the far side. After rain they should be working hard, for this low-lying land waterlogs easily and the drains help to lengthen the time for which the fields can be used. Water in the soil tends to keep it cold and this suppresses plant growth; Drainage makes it warmer earlier which enables the grass to grow sooner in spring.

Pass through the gate and keep to the side of the rhyne.

On rhynes as large as the Wemberham Lane Rhyne there may be swans. These are mute swans with orange bills. The pen (female) has a small, black fleshy knob at the base of her beak while the cob (male) has a much larger one especially in spring. Although they seem common enough birds, their numbers have been depleted in recent years and are only maintained by swans coming from the Continent. The problem is one of lead poisoning. All birds eat small stones to help them with digestion – the stones collect in a muscular bag (gizzard) and grind up the food the bird has swallowed whole or in large lumps. But instead of stones, swans often pick up split-shot dropped by anglers. This, of course, is quickly ground up by the gravel in the gizzard and the lead is absorbed into the bloodstream.

Cob (male) *Pen (female)*

Mute swans
The female has a smaller black fleshy knob at the base of its beak

Lead-poisoned swans can be recognised by a bend in the neck which gradually becomes more acute until the bird finally dies. Anglers and conservationists are now taking this problem seriously and a weight made of an alternative material has been developed – hopefully lead weights will now be phased out.

Pass through the two gates and return to the starting point.

BRENT KNOLL

From the top of Brent Knoll (450 feet high) there are magnificant views in all directions

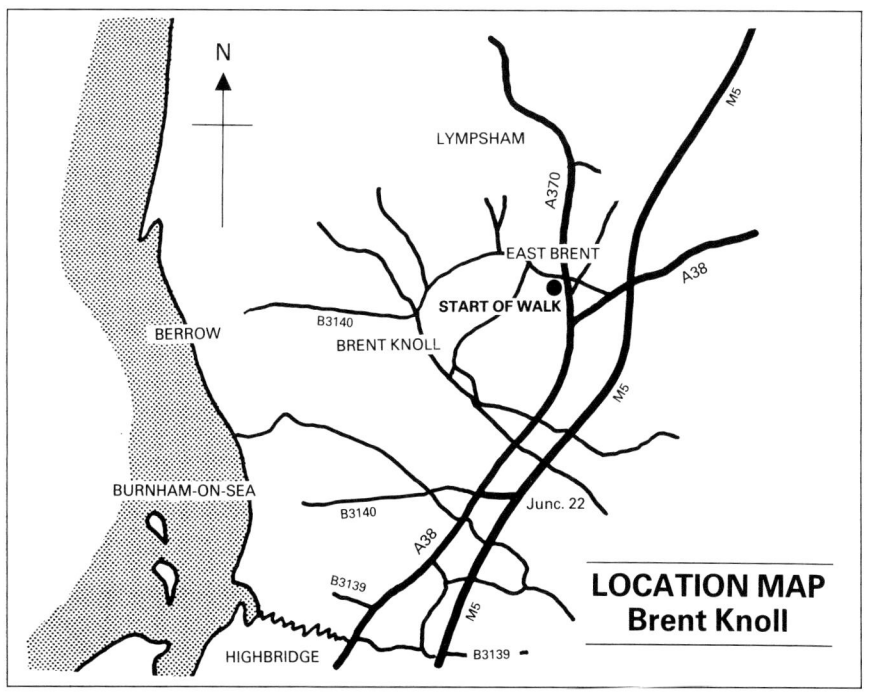

**LOCATION MAP
Brent Knoll**

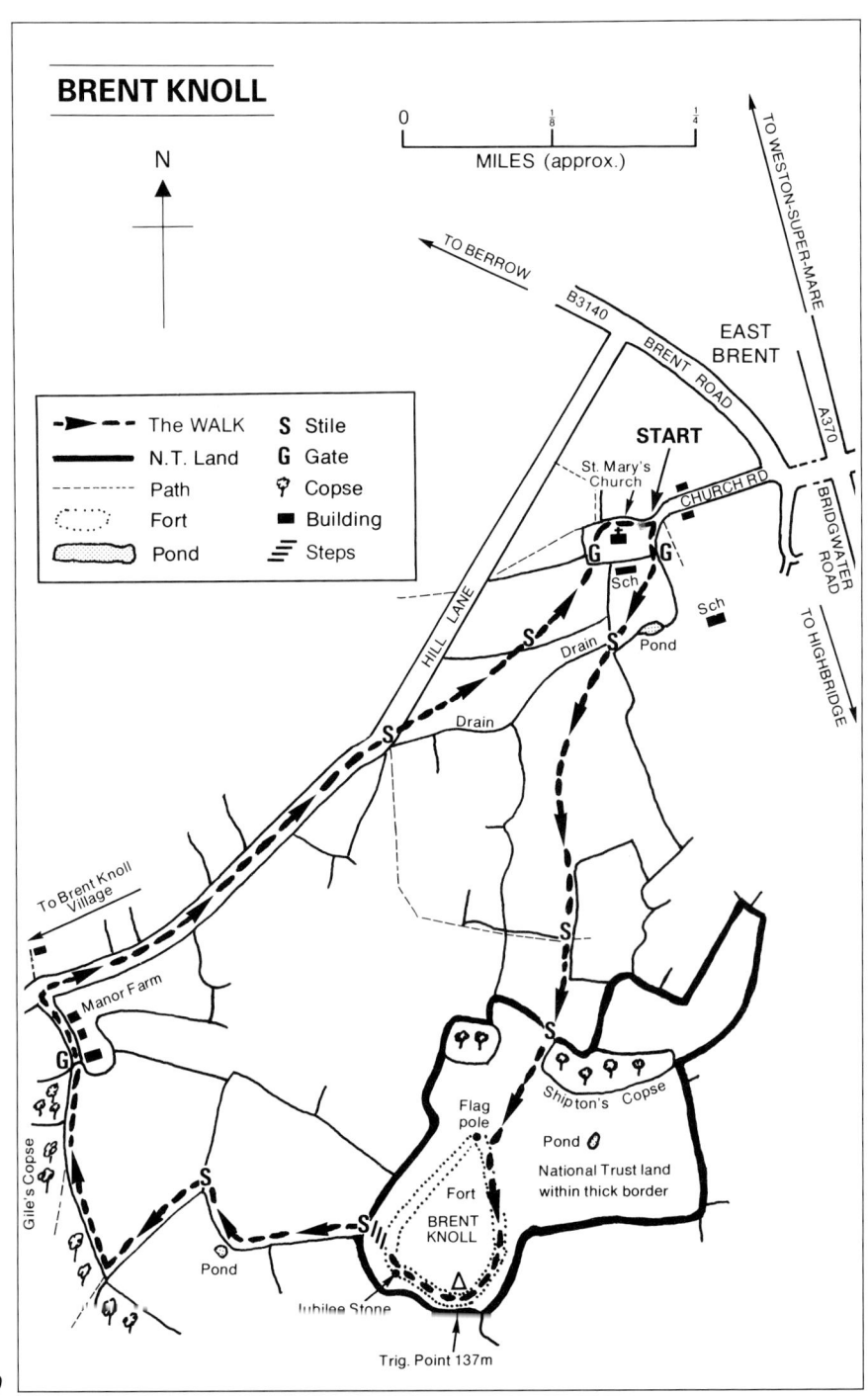

BRENT KNOLL

BRENT KNOLL

Grid Ref. OS 182 (1:50 000) 344 519 Approx. 2 miles

This walk is very steep in places, climbing to 450 feet: nevertheless the views are well worth it. Brent Knoll rises like an island above the surrounding levels and is a well-known local landmark. The short well-nibbled grass is pleasant to walk on and is the main surface encountered. It should be fairly dry even after damp weather.

Walk into the churchyard and turn left before the church. However, a short diversion to the porch and the building itself is worthwhile in order to look for signs of bats.

Some species of bats make extensive use of church buildings because they are cool, dry and often clean. In some porches, bats can find their way into the roof space through quite tiny gaps around the ceiling, but I could find no signs of that here. More likely, at this church, they slip over the door and into the main building itself.

Signs of bats are easy to recognise – they leave small black droppings, a little like those of mice, except that they consist entirely of dried insect remains and will crumble to a powder if compressed. Look for them around the walls, especially in the corners, and on window-sills and seats.

Although there are more species of bats in Britain than any other species of mammal, these tiny animals are becoming increasingly rare. They are totally harmless and exceedingly well adapted to their way of life. Bats eat insects which they catch at night on the wing. Imagine trying to catch moths in woodland after dark with a butterfly net, and one has some idea of the problems bats have to face.

The solution lies in a form of echo-location: they emit from their mouths, or in some cases their noses, high pitched sounds which rebound off objects and are heard by the bats, thus enabling them to avoid colliding with trees and buildings whilst chasing their prey. They catch flying insects either in their mouths or in the sheet of skin stretched between their back legs and their tails.

In winter, when insects are scarce, bats go into hibernation, choosing somewhere cool like a cave or an old railway tunnel to sleep, often bunched together hanging by their feet. Now their temperature falls to that of the surroundings, although never quite to freezing point, and their heart rate slows to around 30 beats a minute. They use very few resources and are usually able to survive on the fat they accumulate in autumn.

A pipistrelle, the smallest British bat, may eat over 3,500 insects a night in summer. At the height of the chase their temperature rises to 42°C and their heart races at 1,000 beats a minute.

Pipistrelle bat

Bats are enormously long lived for their size, and are known to survive for up to 30 years. They have few predators and so, unlike mice and voles which have a short lifespan and a high mortality rate and therefore breed prolifically, female bats average less than one offspring a year throughout their lives. During the last few years, their numbers have fallen dramatically and this comparatively slow rate of replacement means that, even if their difficulties were overcome now, it would be a long time before their population was fully re-established.

Some of the causes for the decline of bats will be seen on this walk. Basically there are two main factors: a loss of habitat for both daytime summer roosts and winter hibernation, and a shortage of food. Because of this, both the animal itself and its home are totally protected by law.

Return to the path and turn right to cross the playground of the village school, then walk diagonally across the field towards the Knoll. Cross the stile and climb the ridge.

Brent Knoll, once known as the Insula Ranarum (Isle of Frogs) is not only an island in the literal sense, rising as it does from the wetlands of the levels, but also in geological terms. It consists of a horizontal strata of Lias limestone and clay and was formed later than the nearby limestone Mendips. Thus, there is no truth in the legend that the hill was one of a number of spadefuls of soil thrown out by the Devil when he was cutting Cheddar Gorge! It is an area extremely rich in fossils and many have been picked up from the fields around the Knoll.

Leaves, flowers and fruit of common privet.

A member of the olive family

Leaves, flowers and fruit of blackthorn.

These are the sloes of sloe gin

Climb the next stile and walk up beside the hedge on the left.

Here, there are many dead elms left by the scourge of Dutch elm disease, and most are now just stumps. Although the felling of such notoriously fickle trees as elms (they tend to drop their branches without warning) is reasonable under the circumstances, it is unfortunate that the removal of old and dying trees has become a modern habit. This general 'tidying up' of the countryside often takes away hollow trees which are potential nesting sites for birds and, perhaps more importantly, would-be roosting places for bats.

The hedge contains a wide variety of hedgerow shrubs including blackthorn, hawthorn, elder and privet. Climbing over it may be black bryony which has shiny heart-shaped leaves and bunches of red berries in autumn. The leaves wither away and leave the poisonous berries strung over the hedge like clumps of red beads on a string.

Cross the stile to the next field entering National Trust land and start to climb the steepest part of the hill.

On the left here is a very steep bank – too steep for agricultural operations – which, as its name of Shipton's Copse suggests, once grew trees. The landowner has thoughtfully replanted this area and the young saplings are protected from the chiselling teeth of rabbits by plastic tree-guards. When they are fully grown they will help to repair the damage to the landscape caused by the death of so many elms.

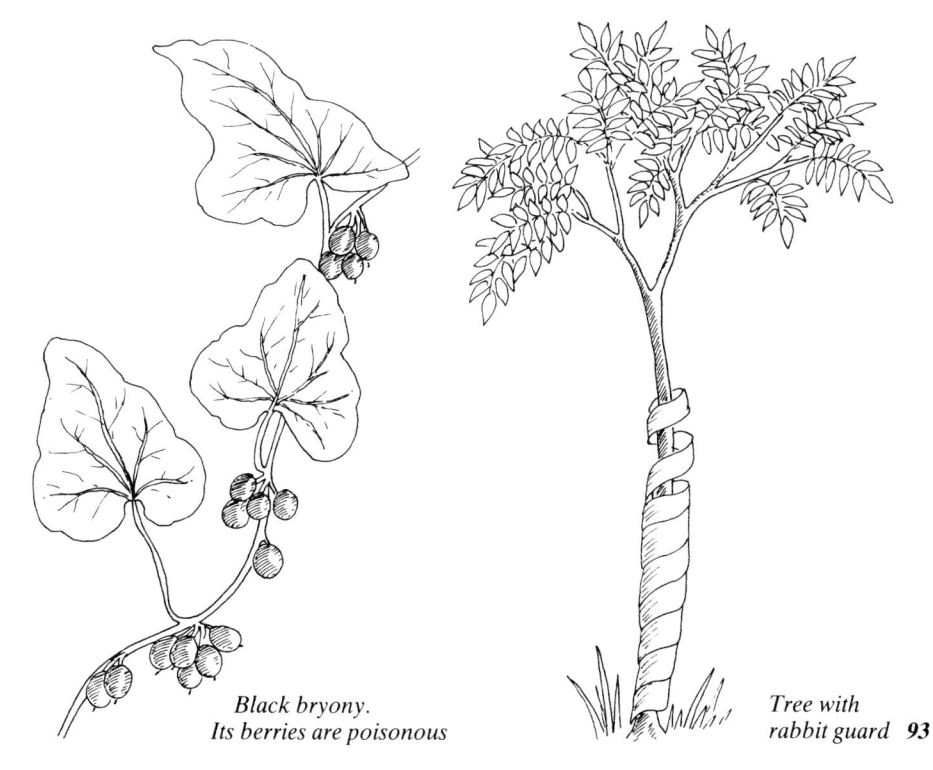

Black bryony.
Its berries are poisonous

Tree with
rabbit guard

The Knoll was acquired in 1979 by The National Trust for Places of Historic Interest or Natural Beauty. This organisation is not connected with the government but is a charity set up in 1895 by three far-sighted Victorians – Octavia Hill, Sir Robert Hunter and the Reverend Hardwicke Rawnsley. The Trust has deliberately shied away from accepting government subsidy in order to preserve its independence and so relies on public donations to purchase and conserve areas like this for the benefit of all.

Climb the steepening slope to the top, pass the flagpole and walk round the summit in a clockwise direction.

From this side there is an excellent view of the motorway which is inescapable because of the surprising amount of noise that rises up the hill from it, even though it is over a mile away. It is interesting to notice just how much land the road occupies, especially at the nearby junction.

The triangulation point OSBM 3357 at 450 feet (137 metres) is a good place to stop and admire the view. You will be by no means the first – Daniel Defoe, author of *Robinson Crusoe,* came here in the seventeenth century and John Wesley visited during the following century.

Looking south east, Glastonbury Tor should be clearly visible. Turning south and then south west will bring into view the Quantocks and Exmoor, the silvery Parrett River snaking into Bridgwater Bay, Burnham-on-Sea with its lighthouse and, immediately beneath, the strip of houses forming Brent Knoll village. These follow the road around the foot of the hill and cling to its lower slopes in order to gain just a few feet of higher ground above the wetness of the levels. Out at sea the twin islands of Steep Holm and Flat Holm can be seen, supposedly two more of the Devil's spadefuls, while, more to the north, the church at Uphill perches on the edge of the quarried cliff fronting Weston-super-Mare. Turning almost a full circle, on the far side of the motorway, the great flank of Crook Peak can be seen; this is, however, the wrong angle from which to view the summit to see how this well-known local landmark gets its name.

As would be expected from such a steep and isolated hill, the top of Brent Knoll has served as a fortress for many over the centuries. Iron-Age men created a hill fort here and remains of their pottery can be seen in Woodspring Museum, Weston-super-Mare; the Romans followed as discoveries of their coins indicate. During Arthurian times, Ider, one of his knights, is said to have killed three giants here. Although there many be some doubts about this, nevertheless it is certain that the summit has been quarried at various times, the most recent digging being during World War II when slit trenches were excavated around the summit plateau for the Home Guard.

The second marker stone records the various beacons and jubilee fires that have been held on this site from 1887 until the present day.

Continue around the hill to the top of the flight of steps.

Before the descent, pause a moment to view Manor Farm, the farmsteading below. The old stone farm buildings lie to the left while the modern grey-roofed and blue-walled construction to the right is a cubicle building. Cattle are kept in during the winter months because it is more convenient to feed them and prevents them churning up the wet pastures with their hooves. Until about 25 years ago, milking cows were kept in a cowshed, each one individually chained up, but then it was found to be cleaner and more efficient to put them in a cubicle house. Here, the cows are free to wander around, to eat silage or perhaps hay, or to lie down in one of the cubicles: individual bedding areas divided up with rails.

The farmer also makes silage: green grass which is preserved by being cut, compacted and sealed to keep the air out – a bit like a tin of peas. The most recent method is to make it into big cylindrical bales and store it individually in black polythene bags. A stack of these bags may be seen at the farm.

Bags of silage

Modern hay is made earlier than meadow hay used to be and silage is made earlier still. Many insects which breed in grassland need all summer to do so and the early cutting of the grass for silage prevents this. Bats, among other species, are thus deprived of an important food source which has contributed to their decline.

Descend the two flights of carefully-constructed steps to the stile. The National Trust has been especially thoughtful here and built a lift gate – a sort of portcullis – for dogs. Dogs must be kept on a lead here as there may be stock on adjacent farmland. Descend the hill keeping close to the hedge on the left.

Just before the first gate in this hedge, honeysuckle is growing – a woody climber which binds spirally in a clockwise direction around any stem within reach. The flowers can be seen all summer but are most noticeable in July and September. They have a delightful fragrance and attract insects, particularly the hawkmoth, which has a long straw-like proboscis with which it sucks in nectar. Hawkmoths are well known for their ability to feed by hovering in front of flowers and inserting their proboscis whilst still airborne.

In autumn, honeysuckle produces lovely red berries with hard pips which are spread by birds eating the flesh. They are not good for humans and tasting them is inadvisable.

Privet hawkmoth feeding on honeysuckle.

This plant has a beautiful scent on summer evenings

Follow the hedge to the bottom corner by the pond and turn right around the field boundary and left over the stile. Keep alongside the hedge on the left.

Extensive use of this area is made by badgers and there is probably a sett nearby. Their age-old paths of pounded earth can be seen leading through the hedge-bottom to the field there where they feed. One of their favourite foods is the earthworm which they seek at night when these creatures come out of their holes to find dead leaves or grasses. Sometimes the badger is able just to pick up worms crawling over the ground in this search. However, it may come across a craftly worm that is seeking food with its head end while leaving its tail safely in the ground ready for a rapid retreat. In this situation, the badger drills down into the ground after its escaping prey, leaving a characteristic excavation three or four inches deep in the turf called a 'snuffle hole'. Snuffle holes often have a swirl of grasses around the top, dragged round by the badger's nose. They are so called because the badger finds it difficult to breath in this situation, perhaps inhaling soil, and snorting and snuffling as a result.

Other badger signs will be old cow-pats flipped over, or clawed through, whilst searching for dung beetles and other insects. Badgers have very long and tough front claws which they use to good effect in this way.

> *The badger marks its territory with 'dung pits' – small depressions containing its rather 'loose' droppings together with secretions from its scent glands. The pits are not covered – which would defeat the purpose – and when full, new ones are dug thus establishing the boundary.*

Turn right along the hedge at the bottom and walk along to the farm. Go through the gate, leaving it either open or shut according to how it was found, and into the yard.

Here, on the right is a range of traditional stone farm buildings with tiles encrusted with lichens and a set of fine steps made from conglomerate stone leading to an upper storey of one of the barns. This stone is often used for steps and I guess it is harder and longer lasting then limestone and less slippery when wet. The buildings here include a cow-shed and open-fronted buildings, few of which are really suited to modern automated agriculture. These days farmers need wide-span multi-purpose buldings into which they can drive tractors, trailers and other machines.

Just before reaching the lane there is a large concrete block on the right, its front edge protected by pieces of metal. It is another relic of a farming practice only relatively recently abandoned; this time connected with the collection of milk. Milk, produced on the farm, was placed in large containers (churns) and left on a churn-stand, such as this one, at a convenient height to be loaded onto the collecting lorry. This vehicle would deliver empty churns and collect full ones before rattling through the lanes to the next farm. Nowadays, the milk produced is stored in a refrigerated tank in the dairy and pumped directly into the bulk milk tanker which calls at the farm every day.

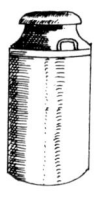

Turn right into the lane.

Milk churn

A short distance along the lane on the left, a new fence runs at right angles to the road which has been erected instead of the hedge that used to grow here. Hedge removal, either to be replaced by fencing or to enlarge fields for greater convenience when using large machines, has been a frequent occurrence in the past 35 years. Unfortunately, it not only removes suitable habitats for birds, mammals and flowers, but has further depleted the insect population, removing breeding and feeding sites and this has had, in turn, serious consequences for bats.

A little further along, on the other side of the lane, privet can be found in the hedge. This is a shrub most frequently found in southern England and is a member of the olive family. It has dull-green leaves which are not fully evergreen and fall by spring. The privet flower grows in white spikes and has a very sweet scent and the fruit is a black berry containing two seeds. When I walked along here there was an old milk churn in the right-hand hedge. Now that these are no longer required for transporting milk, they have been turned to other tasks and this one seemed to be used to block a hole in the hedge. In the field nearly, a large and fine willow tree stands over a field pond. Once a frequent feature of farms, these ponds are also becoming a rarity, depriving populations of amphibians and insects of breeding sites, and causing the common frog to become far from common and leading to the protection, by law, of the great crested newt.

Magpies are often here – rather smart members of the crow family. With long tails, plumage that is black, white and iridescent blue, and a harsh cackling call, they are unmistakable birds that have long been associated

> *Magpies, if they detect danger from an owl or cat perhaps, will mob an animal unmercifully, cackling away in very loud cries.*

with a variety of superstitions. They are true omnivores, eating both insects and seeds, and in spring rob the nests of small birds of the eggs and chicks. Magpies build a domed-shaped nest, a little larger than a football, often constructed with thorny twigs.

Magpies

Piratical collectors of shiny objects

As the next bend is rounded, a stile will be seen with two white bars. Climb over it and cross the field aiming slightly to the right of the elm stump in the hedge and the church beyond. At the top of the rise in the field will be seen the white end of another stile – make for this. Climb the stile and walk towards the church spire.

This spire had great significance in the past for guiding ships. The Knoll is clearly visible from the sea and from a distance looks like an island itself. It is claimed that before the Burnham-on-Sea lighthouses were built in 1829 and 1832, the spire of East Brent church was regularly whitewashed to guide ships into Burnham – there is, however, no sign of this now.

Approaching the kissing gate into the churchyard, a number of sycamore trees will be seen to the left on the boundary between the gate and the field. This is a member of the maple family and was introduced from France in the middle ages. A very quick and successful grower, it has invaded a number of woodlands, taking over as other trees have died or been removed. Unlike the native oak which provides a home for other species numbering in excess of 200, the sycamore can provided for a paltry 25 and is considered by many conservationists to be a weed. The tree has distinctive five-lobed leaves, yellowish flowers hanging in clusters and hard brown seeds which grow in pairs and each has a wing on which it whirls as it falls to earth. In spite of its poor reputation, it is very hardy and grows where other trees fail, being successful in habitats ranging from polluted cities to windswept coasts.

Pass through the kissing gate and walk round the church, with its large yews, back down to the village.

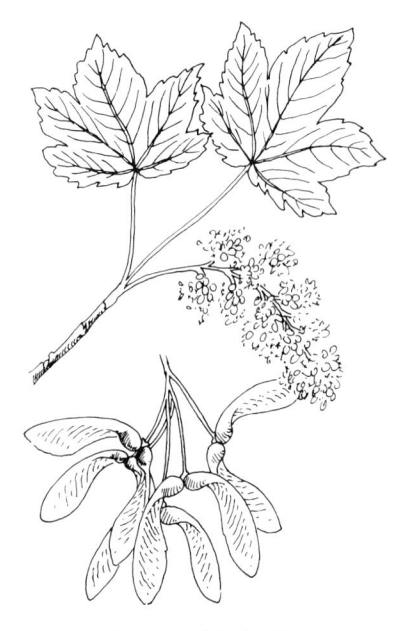

Leaves, flowers and fruit of sycamore   *Yew branch and berries*

BERROW

The beach at Berrow is a good place to find animal tracks

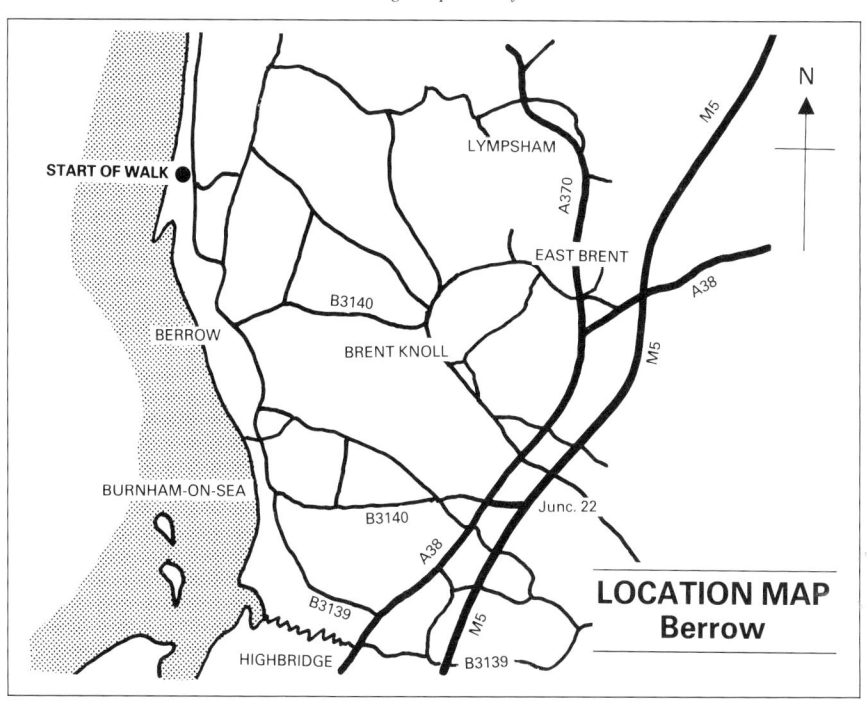

**LOCATION MAP
Berrow**

BERROW

N

BERROW FLATS

Posts
Toilets   Toilets
VEHICULAR ACCESS
Caravan Park
Unity Farm
Sand Dunes
Footpath
Rough Grassland
Footpath
Sand Dunes
Sand Dunes
Footpath
Rough Grassland
Caravan Park
Sand Dunes
COAST ROAD
To Brean

Legend:
- ➤ ─ ─ The WALK
- ⭘ Sand Dunes
- ─ ─ ─ Path
- \\\\\\ Rough Grassland
- ▓ Pond

0   1/8   1/4
MILES (approx.)

START
Car Parking
POSTS
FOOTPATH ACCESS
Bus Stop
Caravan Park
HURN LANE

Rough Grassland
Golf Links
Sand Dunes
Golf Links
Drain
Sand Dunes

BRISTOL CHANNEL
Tide Line
Tide Line

Sand Dunes
Golf Links
Pond
Sand Dunes
Pond
Golf Links
St Mary's Church
Footpath

Mead Farm
To Burnham-on-Sea & Weston-super-Mare
Berrow Manor
BERROW

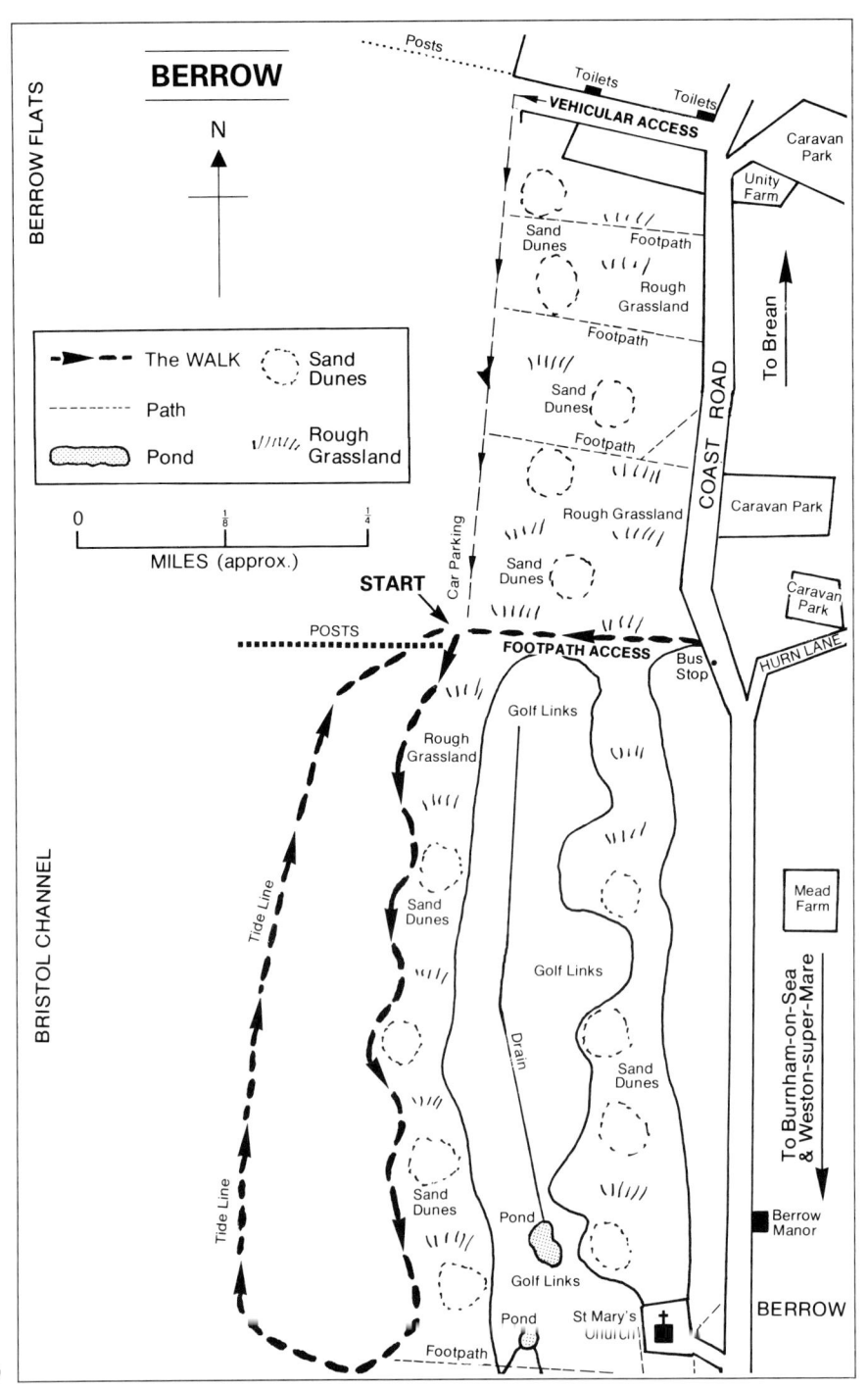

100

BERROW

Grid Ref. OS 182 (1:50 000) 293 534　　　　　　　　　　　Approx. 1½ miles

This is a walk along a sandy beach of the nicest kind. I have been here when the sand has been almost too hot for bare feet and also when the ice has been piled up on the beach in great parallel banks, each marking a successive tide. The notes for this walk are slightly different from the others in the book. Although I suggest keeping to the top of the beach on the outward journey and returning along the tide line, I have not pointed to any specific place to look for any particular species. This is because the area is being moulded all the time by wind and water and changes quickly and easily – in any case, one sand dune look much like another! I have tried to give a broad guide to things to look for and what is found depends upon the hour, the season, the weather and the walker's powers of observation. Although the route covers about one and a half miles, a longer walk can be taken if required.

If driving enter the beach at the first vehicular access on the left going north, and turn left along the sands. Leave the vehicle at the row of posts which runs down the beach (see map). If on foot there is public footpath access opposite Hurn Lane.

One of the most interesting times to visit this beach is early on a spring or summer morning, as this is when animal tracks are at their best. (See pages 118–119 for illustrations of some animal tracks.) Choose a still morning so that loose sand will not have filled the prints, arrive before other visitors have disturbed the ground, and come when the sun is still fairly low so that its long rays will cast shadows and reveal the form of the tracks.

It is surprising the number of different animals which visit the beach. The fox trots through the dunes or walks along the strandline seeking carrion (such as dead gulls washed up by the tide or the remains of yesterday's picnics) or perhaps hunting for rabbits or smaller mammals. Its fine four-toed track makes a trail in a line down the sand as if the animal was walking an invisible tightrope. If the trail is followed it may be evident where the fox has sat down on the sand or maybe dug up a rabbit stop (a shallow nursery burrow in which the doe rabbit hides her young). If a predator discovers the stop, the young rabbits will be excavated and consumed, leaving a small hole and a pile of nesting material. Often the best tracks are made when an animal with sandy feet has walked on mud, as the dry dusty paws leave perfectly-formed prints which, in the case of the fox show the long hairs growing between the toes. The badger's track is much broader with five toes. It has none of the daintiness of that of the fox which, like a dog, walks on tip-toes. The badger is plantigrade like a human and walks on flat feet, and in mud or damp sand the marks of its long claws, especially those on the fore feet, can be seen very easily.

> *Badger tracks can be confusing for when walking or trotting, the badger places its hind feet partially or wholly in the tracks of its fore feet resulting in a confusing line of tracks with seven or eight toes to each footprint.*

Rabbits come down here too. They like seaside living because of the grasses just inland and the soft sand in which to burrow. Their tracks look a little like a pair of exclamation marks printed side by side ! ! and in spite of first appearances, the rabbit making these would be hopping up the page and not down it. It is quite common to find a rabbit skull among the sand where the animal has been killed or has died of disease. (See page 117 for illustration). The body may have been buried by sand or picked clean by scavengers until only the bones remain. The skeleton then breaks up and is scattered, the most recognisable remaining feature being the skull but without the lower jaw. Invariably the base of the skull disappears too, revealing the brain cavity. Look for the small sockets which once contained teeth behind the two incisors – one of the features that distinguishes rabbits and hares from rodents.

Hedgehogs may come down onto the beach leaving a trail of five-toed tracks which look like small human hand prints. These prickly insectivores will look for food of various types and find the soft sand areas especially lucrative as many insects and other invertebrates become trapped in pits in the sand and find it impossible to climb up the tiny moving grains forming the sides. Keep a look out, too, for the delicate trails left by small creatures like caterpillars, beetles, weevils and millipedes.

Two animals unexpectedly found in such a hot and dry environment are the frog and the toad. Close to Berrow Church there are ponds on the golf links and also fresh water near the top of the beach and as a consequence these amphibians have been found on the sands. Both species leave feathery tracks especially the toad which crawls rather than hops.

If here before sunrise the dawn will be chilly at first, and the warmth the sun brings will be welcome as it climbs over the horizon and its life-giving glow flows onto the sand. If it is high summer, the cool of the dawn may soon be wished for as the heat, reflecting off the light-toned sand, turns this place into a mini-Sahara.

> *The tides ebb and flow in response to the phases of the moon. Every month there are spring tides (a large distance between high and low water) and neap tides (a small distance). The highest tides of all occur at the equinoxes – around 21 March and 21 September every year.*

Common toad

Its warty skin conceals poisonous glands which make it distasteful if bitten

In early summer there will be a surprising variety of plants flowering along the top of the beach and in the dunes. If the beach is departed from, walk in the gullies between the dunes keeping off the sand-dune faces, as climbing these can cause serious erosion. The dunes here are held together by the roots of plants growing on them and once these plants are worn away by trampling feet, or the sand around them is removed, the roots lose their grip and the sand, with nothing to hold it, begins to shift. On a windy day it is easy to see this happening; Weston-super-Mare, for instance, acquires sand-drifts on its sea-front roads after an onshore gale. In order to prevent this erosion many seaside authorities carry out dune-restoration works, which generally come in two parts. The first objective is to slow the wind down, as below a certain speed the current of air will drop its burden of sand. Many methods have been tried and the most usual is to form a windbreak about two-feet high, around which the sand builds up during windy periods. Having got the sand where it is wanted, the second stage is to keep it there and for this marram grass it generally used.

Marram is one of three dune grasses, all to be found here, that share similar features for dealing with the conditions imposed by the environment. The dunes nearest the sea are the richest in nutrients (obtained from decomposing material swept in by the tide) and in calcium from pulverised sea shells.

The rain washes these materials out quite quickly and so the further from the beach, the poorer the growing capacity of the dune sand. At the same time, those dunes nearest the sea are the most exposed to salt either carried on the wind or in the form of spray and so greater salt resistance is required by plants growing near the beach. The dunes closest to the sea tend to grow sea couch grass, the middle zone supports lyme grass, and marram grass grows on the so-called 'white dunes' furthest away from the shore.

All three grasses are able to withstand inundation by sand by growing underground shoots which find their way to the surface even after the harshest storm. Marram grass can grow through a metre of sand when necessary. The dry nature of their desert-like home has also led them to evolve ways of conserving water. On hot dry days their leaves roll up to form tubes to prevent loss of moisture, unrolling during damper times when the danger is past.

Another dune-stabilising plant grows here in profusion – the sea buckthorn which has a mesh of roots to hold the sand and leathery grey-green leaves to retain moisture. Thorns protect the shrub still further and make it a useful nesting site for small birds. In autumn it produces vitamin-rich orange berries.

A frail-looking yellow flower is also to be found here throughout the summer – the evening primrose which produces a flower about two inches in diameter on a stem more than two-feet tall. Originally introduced from North America, it has spread prolifically on sand dunes and waste areas. True to its name, the evening primrose opens on balmy evenings to allow moths to pollinate it.

Marram grass helps bind sand dunes   *Evening primrose*

Another yellow flower, not exclusively found on dunes and considered by farmers to be a menace, is ragwort. Its ragged leaves, from which it takes its name, are the favourite food of the caterpillars of the cinnabar moth. The plant is a member of the daisy family and grows up to four-feet tall. It is mildly poisonous to cattle, though not apparently to sheep and certainly not to those caterpillars. The black and yellow-striped larvae will eat the leaves down to the stalk and, having reduced the plant to a skeleton, will climb down to the ground and search for another. The adult moth is generally included among the tiger moth family and is a day-flying species. It is crimson and black in colour which probably indicates that it is distasteful to would-be predators.

Cinnabar moths and caterpillar on a ragwort plant

Sea spurge should also be discovered along the top of the shore – it is typical of the spurge family whose members are found in many different habitats. It possesses what looks like a green flower which, instead of petals or sepals, has the male and female parts of the plant cupped in bracts that are actually modified leaves.

Near Berrow Church, the tower of which can be seen from the beach, are a number of reed beds. The reeds themselves look beautiful as their silver feathery heads wave and shimmer in the sun and, in spring, reed warblers may be heard singing from them.

This is as good a place as any to turn around, but the walk can be extended for a good distance if wished.

Bridgwater Bay extends to the south and west from here and is well known for its profusion of wading birds. These can often be seen feeding at the edge of the incoming tide and a good time to visit is when the tide is creeping in over the broad expanse of mud that forms the estuary of the Parrett River.

Bridgwater Bay is an internationally recognised area for ducks and waders. Its miles of mud flats, which are exposed at low tide and have been declared a National Nature Reserve by the Nature Conservancy Council, attract large numbers of water-fowl especially during migratory periods in spring and autumn.

Sanderlings are common, especially in spring and autumn, as many of these birds use Britain as a stopping-off point to stock up with food when travelling to their Arctic breeding grounds from Africa or vice versa. They are small, grey and white with a distinctive white wing-bar in flight. The most common characteristic, however, is their rushing and scurrying behaviour as they dart here and there along the tide line searching for food.

Even more numerous at certain times of the year are dunlins, and in February there can be over two thousand here. In summer they can be recognised by their black belly which is a certain give-away while in winter they may be a lot more difficult to differentiate from others in the sandpiper family such as the sanderling. They have a longer slightly down-curved bill and a less-pronounced wing stripe in flight. It is when in flight, though, that dunlin come into their own. They have been compared often to a plume of smoke but I find them more mysterious than that. The grey backs and white bellies of their winter plumage make them seem to appear and disappear as if by magic, when they wheel and turn against a white sky, and their aerobatic flight is beautiful to watch.

Sanderling in winter plumage

Dunlin in summer plumage

Two other waders that may be seen here are the curlew and the oyster catcher. The latter is readily distinguishable from other waders by its comparatively large size, long orange bill, pink legs, and black and white plumage which has earned it the nickname of 'sea pie'. They may be seen in small groups or perhaps just a single bird probing in the mud with its beak. Oyster catchers make a high-pitched 'kleep kleep' alarm call but rarely fly very far if frightened when feeding, landing again a little further along the shore.

When feeding on cockles or mussels oyster catchers either stab or hammer them open. The chicks learn one of these methods from their parents adopting it to the exclusion of the other. The bills of 'hammering' oyster catchers invariably become damaged thus rendering them less effective when seeking other types of prey.

Oyster catcher

Curlew

Finally there is the curlew, Britain's largest wading bird. It has speckled-brown plumage and an easily-recognisable down-curved bill with which it probes in the mud for food. The bill of the female can be up to one-third longer than that of the male. The other major distinguishing feature is the bird's call of 'coorli' from which it takes its name – a haunting cry which reminds me of wide open marshes or moors, for this bird breeds inland. Like other waders, it nests on the ground laying camouflaged eggs to prevent discovery. Its chicks can leave the nest and run around on the ground with their parents almost as soon as they have hatched. If they feel endangered, the chicks will flatten themselves against the earth, stretching their heads and necks out and keeping still and silent while the parents try to draw the unwanted attentions of the predator away from them.

Walk back along the strand line: the line comprising seaweed and other detritus brought in by the sea and stranded on the beach. The best time to do this is after a storm with an onshore wind, possibly combined with a high tide. All sorts of debris will be found tangled up with the mass of dark weed on the beach; many of the objects are man-made. Wooden items are frequent

> *Shelduck breed in this area. Unlike other duck species, the female is as brightly coloured as the male and so, in order to remain concealed when incubating the eggs, they build a nest underground often in a disused rabbit burrow.*

Male *Female* *Shelduck*

and may range from a complete fish box to a broom head or the broken handle of a canoe paddle. Increasingly, nowadays, plastics are washed up onto the beach and old bottles, broken toys and bits of fish net are common. Some, like the net, are dangerous and may catch around the legs of a gull or the neck of a seal with fatal results. Such plastic items sometimes carry their own complement of wildlife. I once found a dustbin lid on the beach complete with a small group of stalked (goose) barnacles attached to its underside. Following a period of south-westerly gales, the lid had arrived, probably from the South Atlantic, with a number of 'passengers'. These animals were still alive, though most items discovered during beachcombing will be skeletons or egg cases.

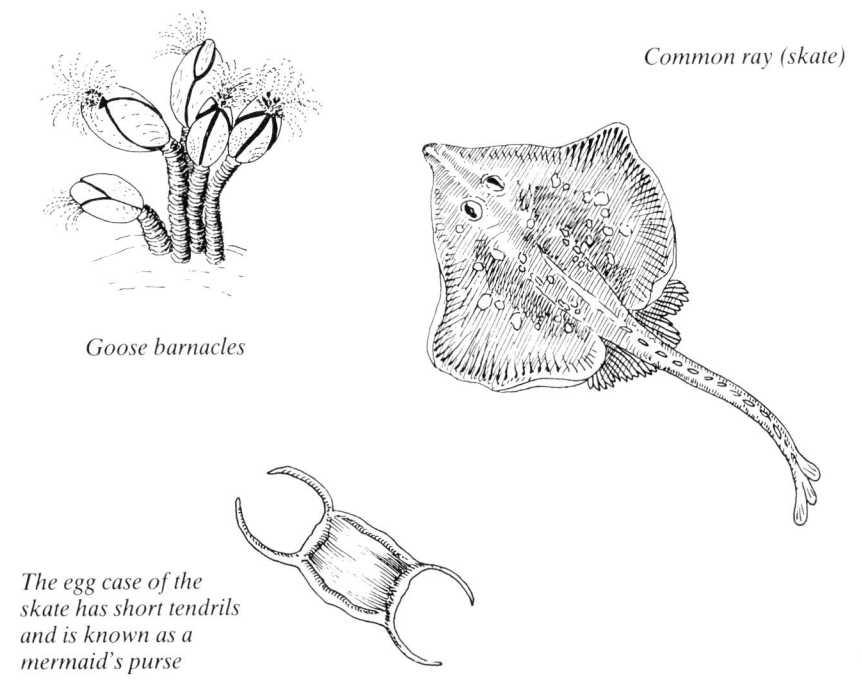

Common ray (skate)

Goose barnacles

The egg case of the skate has short tendrils and is known as a mermaid's purse

The majority of animals living on the seashore have exoskeletons: skeletons which, unlike humans, are on the outside of the bodies like crabs, cockles and so on. The bones that are found are in the form of shells and can vary from long razor shells, through snail-like winkle and whelk shells, the shells of limpets, to those of cockles and mussels which come in matching pairs connected by a hinge of tissue unless broken apart by the waves. (See illustrations on page 120.) Egg cases are quite common, especially those of the whelk (a light bubbly mass) and of the skate, which is a dry dark case with a strand at each corner and is colloquially known as a mermaid's purse. A variety of crab shells may also be found, or the bone of a cuttlefish like that which is given to budgies. The really exciting thing about beachcombing is that, like natural history, one never knows what might turn up next.

Make the way back to the start.

Lesser spotted dog fish egg cases with long tendrils.
These are also called mermaid's purses

KEYS TO IDENTIFYING WILDLIFE

Unfortunately space does not permit the inclusion of a key to all the species that may be seen on these wildlife walkabouts. Instead, the following notes have been set out on the particular features to look for if a species is encountered that is not recognised. These notes should help the walker to jot down the important clues which will be a guide to correct identification when reference books at home or at the public library are consulted. It is even better if field guides are taken on walks – a flower guide is especially useful as it will help to resist any temptation to take a specimen away, which, apart from destroying the pleasure of others, is very likely to be against the law. A notebook and pencil are invaluable on any walk.

The following pages contain notes on:

Birds – general identification points
– beak types
– feet types

Plants – general identification points

Ferns – general points
– illustrations

Trees – general identification points
– illustrations of bud, leaf, flower and fruit of horse chestnut tree

Mammals – general identification points
– fur on wire
– hazel nut clues
– skulls and bones
– animal tracks

Sea shells – general points
– illustrations

Insects and Spiders – general rules
– illustrations

BIRDS

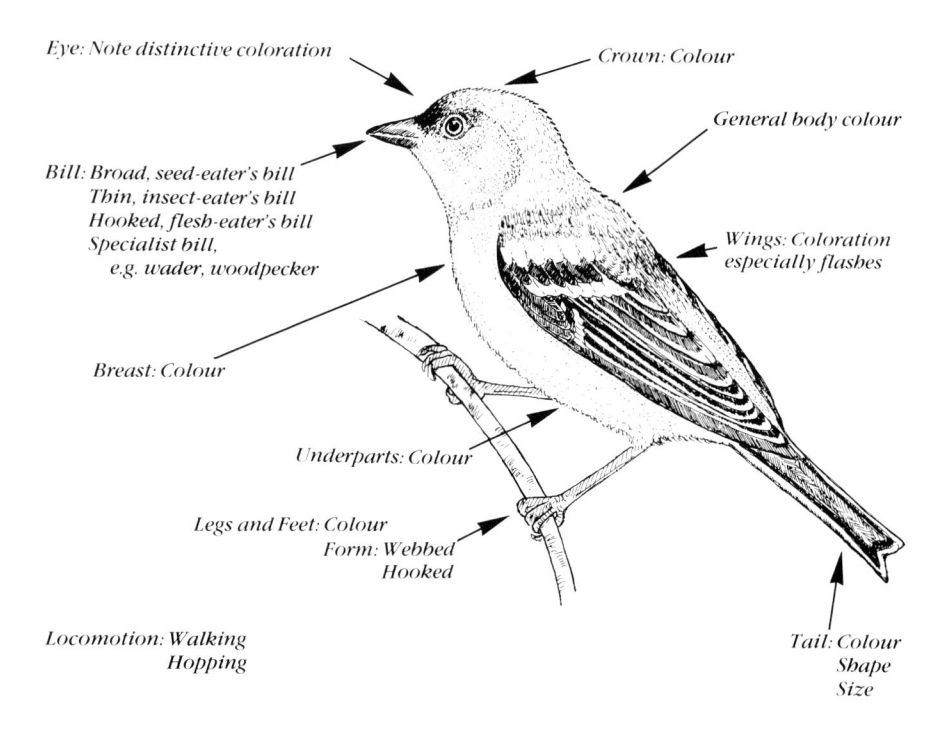

Eye: Note distinctive coloration

Crown: Colour

General body colour

Bill: Broad, seed-eater's bill
Thin, insect-eater's bill
Hooked, flesh-eater's bill
Specialist bill,
  e.g. wader, woodpecker

Wings: Coloration especially flashes

Breast: Colour

Underparts: Colour

Legs and Feet: Colour
Form: Webbed
Hooked

Locomotion: Walking
Hopping

Tail: Colour
Shape
Size

Size: In relation to say a blackbird or starling.

Habitat: Where seen, e.g. arable land; coniferous woodland.

Activities: Feeding on the ground, clinging to tree-trunk, etc.

Time of year.

Area of country.

Sounds: Turn them into words, if possible, e.g. cer-loo (curlew call).

Behaviour: e.g. feeding continuously; short run, feed, short run.

Flight: Flight pattern – dipping, hovering, soaring, etc.
  Speed
  Altitude
  Purposeful or localised – hunting insects, fish, or displaying, etc.
  Shape of wings – rounded, pointed, swept back, etc.

Water birds:
  Swimming and diving for some time
  Swimming and bobbing under
  Swimming and upturning with head under and tail in air
  Diving from branch or air.

BIRDS' BEAKS

Broadly speaking, small birds can be divided into two types by their bills. Those with fine slim beaks are insect-eaters while seed-eaters have broader, more powerful, bills. There are, however, a large number of specialist feeders who have evolved beaks of a shape suited to their diet. Flesh-eaters have hooked beaks for tearing their prey, waders have long beaks for probing sand and mud, and ducks have flat bills for seiving their food from the water.

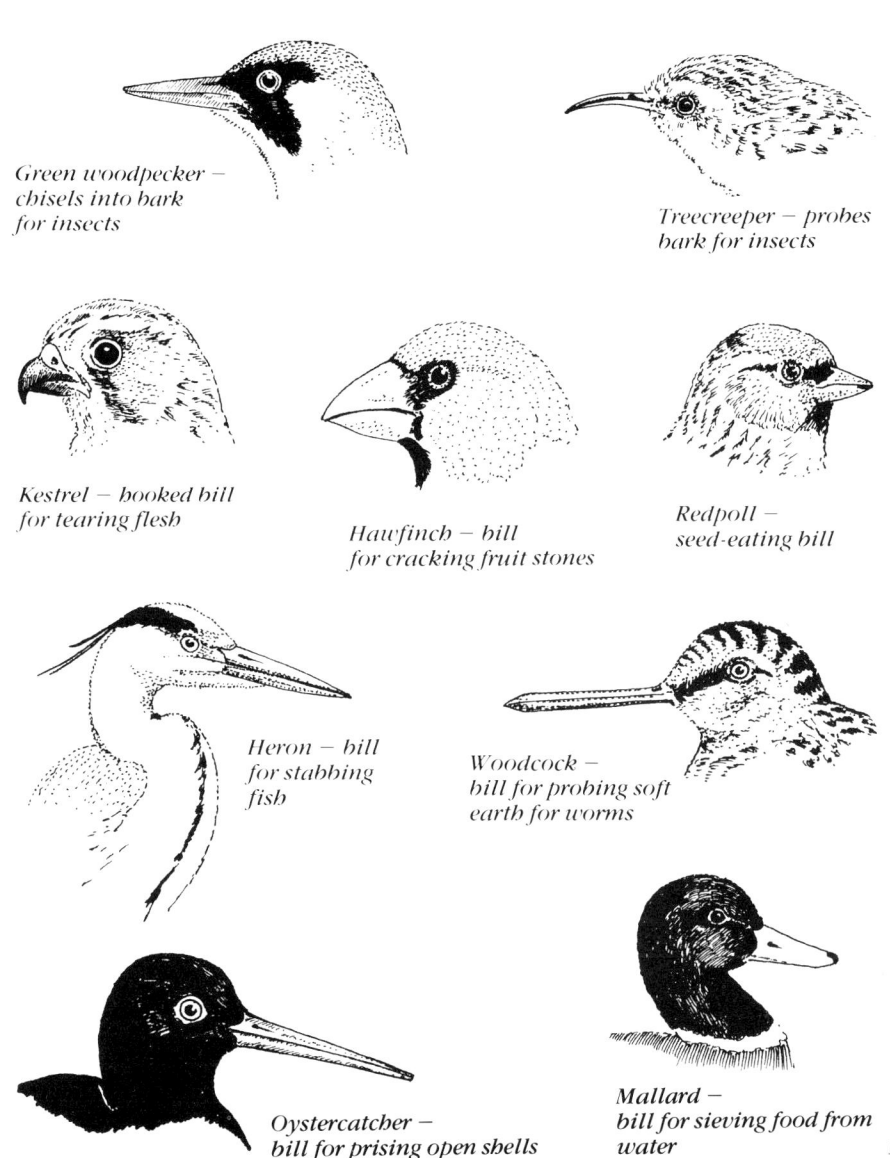

Green woodpecker – chisels into bark for insects

Treecreeper – probes bark for insects

Kestrel – hooked bill for tearing flesh

Hawfinch – bill for cracking fruit stones

Redpoll – seed-eating bill

Heron – bill for stabbing fish

Woodcock – bill for probing soft earth for worms

Oystercatcher – bill for prising open shells

Mallard – bill for sieving food from water

BIRDS' FEET

The more specialist birds have evolved feet to suit their habits and environment, e.g. the webbed feet of water birds which enable them to swim quickly. This specialism tends to make water birds much slower on land and the more aquatic their lifestyle, the less mobile thay are out of water and in extreme cases, such as divers, they can hardly walk. At the other end of the scale are coots and moorhens – equally adapted to moving on land and in water. Their feet have lobes on the toes to increase their width when swimming and yet enable them to run unhindered.

Other birds with specialist feet include the predators which have sharp claws for seizing their prey. Woodpeckers have two toes facing forwards and two backwards which allows them to cling to vertical tree trunks with their feet holding the bark in a clamp-like grip.

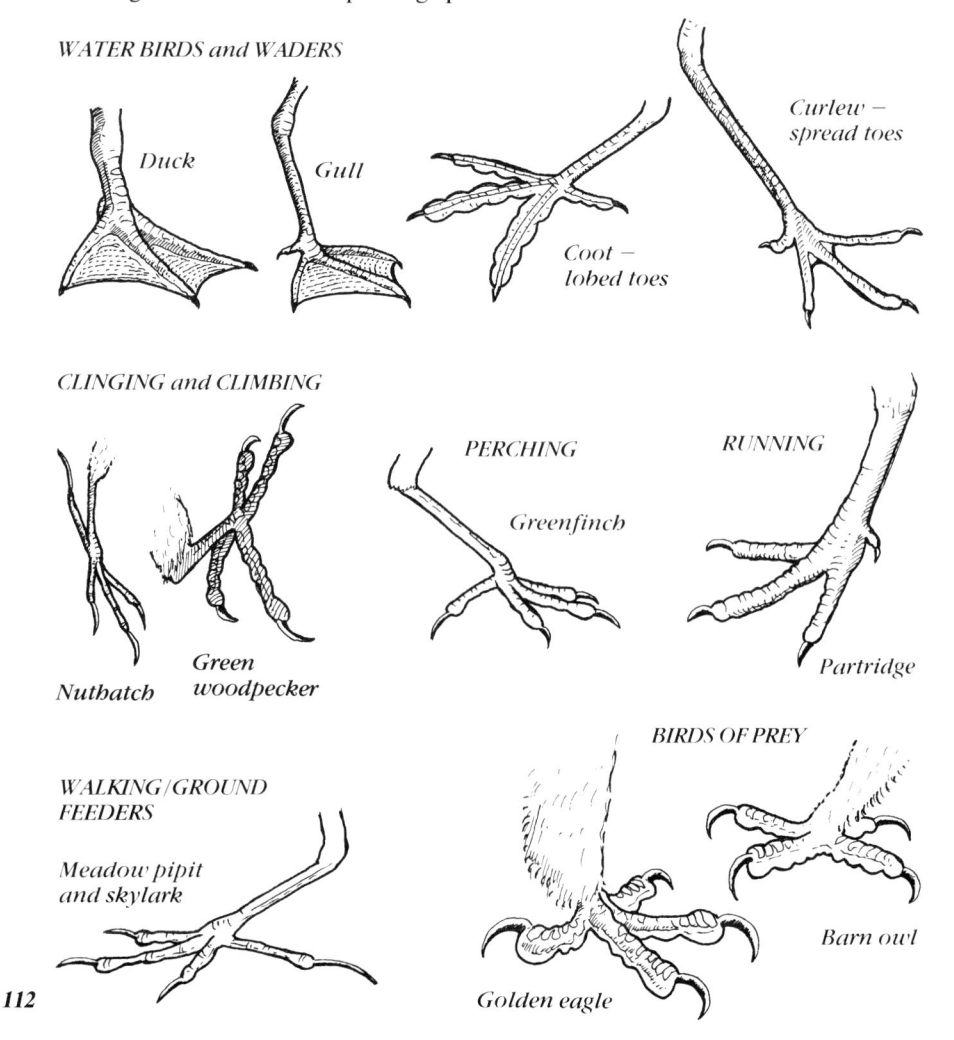

WATER BIRDS and WADERS

Duck

Gull

Coot – lobed toes

Curlew – spread toes

CLINGING and CLIMBING

Nuthatch

Green woodpecker

PERCHING

Greenfinch

RUNNING

Partridge

WALKING/GROUND FEEDERS

Meadow pipit and skylark

BIRDS OF PREY

Golden eagle

Barn owl

PLANTS

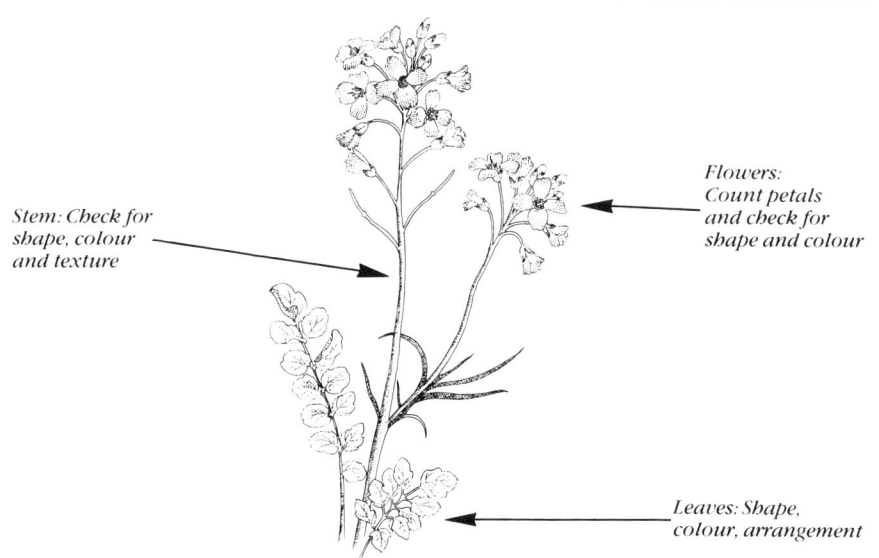

Stem: Check for shape, colour and texture

Flowers: Count petals and check for shape and colour

Leaves: Shape, colour, arrangement

Flowers:
    Colour
    General shape: e.g. 'traditional flower'
                      composite flower like the dandelion
                      asymmetrical like the foxglove
    Number of petals, petal shape – rounded, pointed, toothed, etc.
    Arrangement – single flower on stalk, clustered, several clusters, etc.
    Size of flower
    Scent.

Stem:
    Cross-sectional shape: gauge by feel
    Texture: smooth, hairy, prickly, etc.
    Height
    Colour.

Leaves:
    Arrangement on stem
    Edges toothed, saw edged, smooth, convoluted, etc.
    Veins – prominent, different colour, etc.
    Peculiar coloration
    Texture – hairy, dull, shiny, etc.

Seeds: Colour, size, how dispersed.

Environment: Chalk, limestone area, moorland, etc.

Habitat: Hedgerow bottom, stream bank, limestone paving, peat bog, hazel wood, etc.

Time of year.

FERNS

Ferns are primitive flowerless green plants whose ancestors formed present-day coal deposits. On the undersides of fern fronds are brown circular discs which are groups of spore sacs. Either wind or animals disperse the tiny spores, which are released when the sacs split, and from each spore grows a small green disc containing both the male and female parts of the plant. It needs a film of rainwater to enable the sperms to travel to the female egg sacs for fertilisation to occur, and this requirement for a moist climate means that ferns are more common in the humid west of Britain. The illustrations are not to scale.

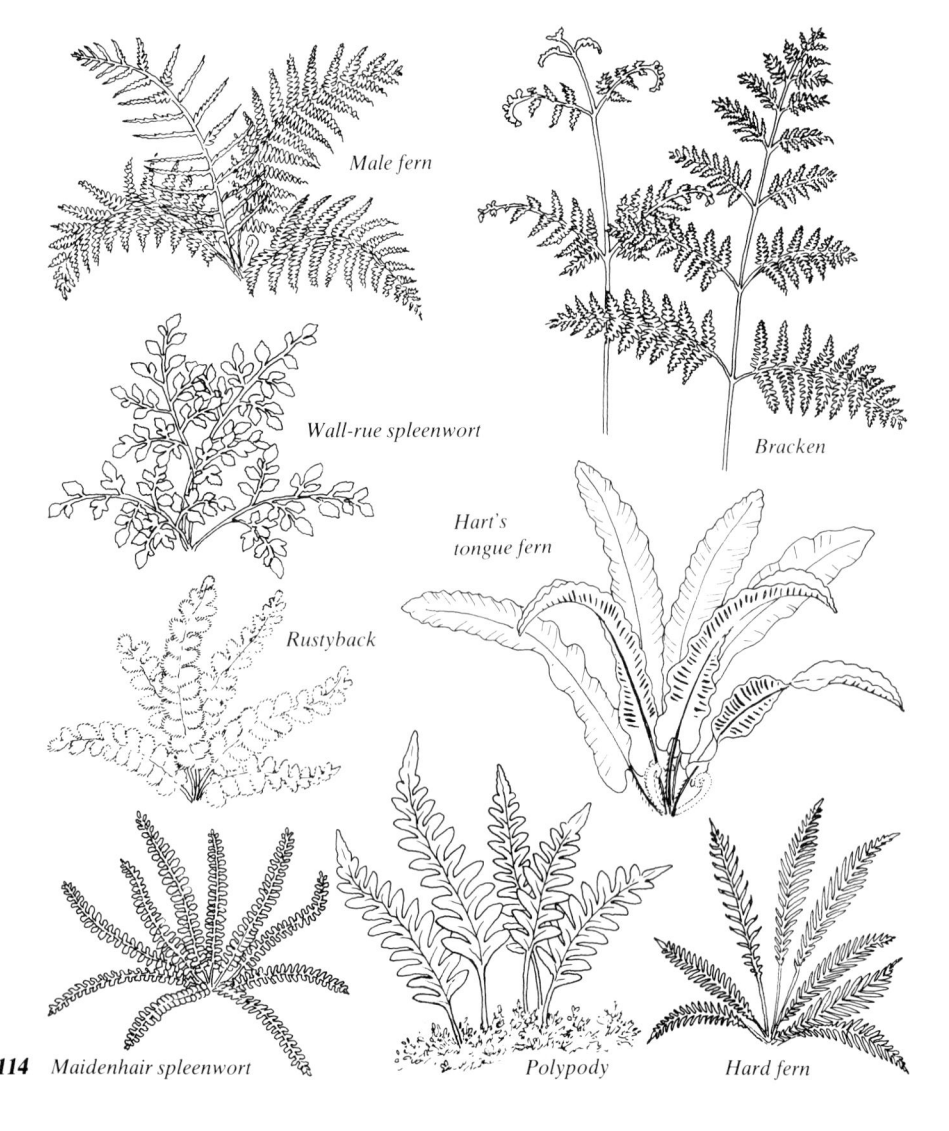

Male fern

Bracken

Wall-rue spleenwort

Hart's tongue fern

Rustyback

Maidenhair spleenwort

Polypody

Hard fern

TREES

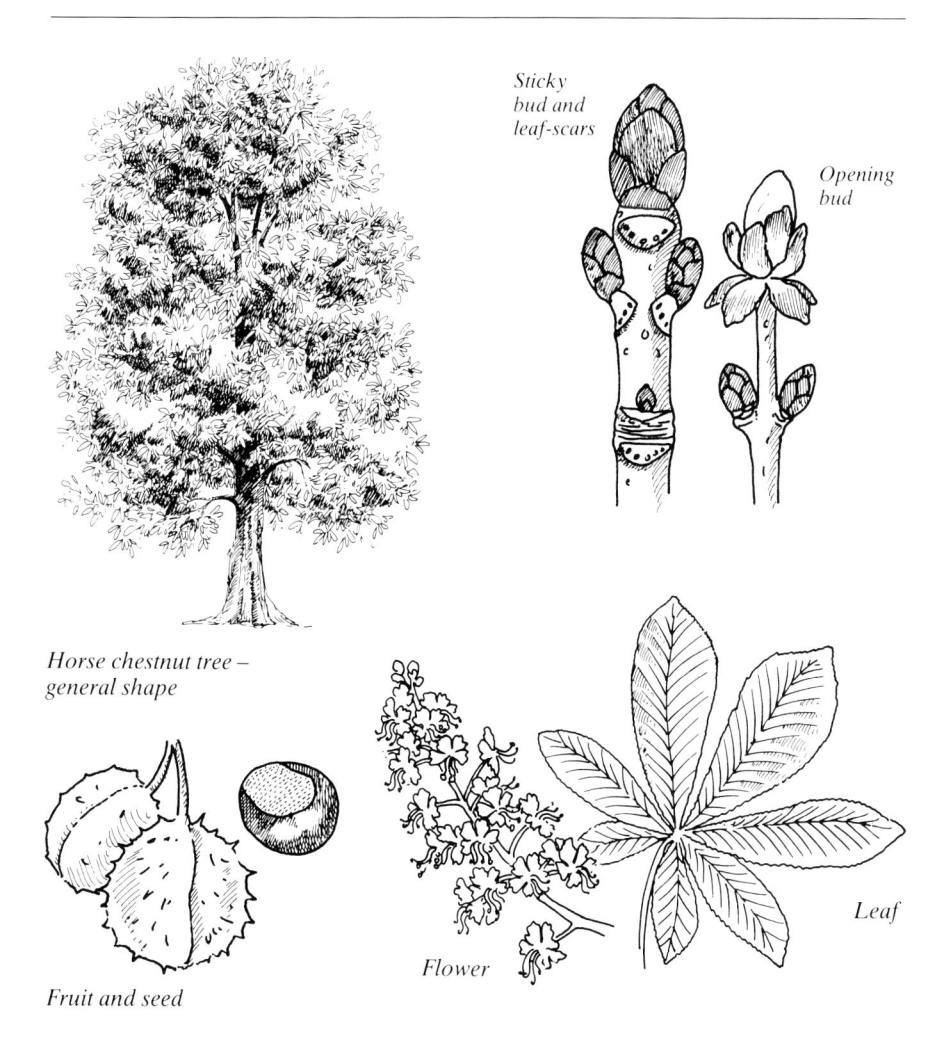

Sticky bud and leaf-scars

Opening bud

Horse chestnut tree – general shape

Fruit and seed

Flower

Leaf

General shape and branch shape: Drooping, elbowed, etc.

Height: e.g. in relation to the height of a normal telegraph pole.

Location: Near to, or in woodland, etc.

Soil type.

Bark: Colour, texture, flaking, peeling, fissured, smooth, etc.

Leaves: Colour, shape, size, veins, grouped or single, deciduous or evergreen.

Flowers: Colour, shape, form, time of year.

Fruits or seeds: Shape, form, colour, time of year.

MAMMALS

Apart from squirrels and the occasional rabbit, it is unlikely that many mammals will be seen unless the walker rises early and moves very quietly. On the other hand tracks and signs may be seen. If a mammal is encountered, here are some tips to help with identification, and to sort out some common mistakes.

Hare: Large, gingery orange; generally solitary; fast runner.

Rabbit: Smaller, grey with conspicuous tail; often in groups; lives in holes.

Rat: Pointed snout; pink and hairless ears and tail.

Water vole: Blunt snout; furry ears and tail; dives readily; aquatic habitat.

Deer: Almost certainly the only deer to be seen locally will be a roe deer. Usually solitary with reddish-gingery coat and knobbly antlers on the buck.

Otter: Very rare; rich-brown fur; nocturnal; larger than a cat.

Mink: Quite common and may be seen in daylight; dark chocolate-brown; smaller that a cat.

Shrew: Very active; very small; long quivering pointed nose.

Vole: Blunt nose; furry ears and tail; slower moving; very short tail.

Mouse: Pointed nose; naked ears and tail which is very long; quick bouncing like a miniature kangaroo.

Stoat: Larger than weasel – nearly 18″ (46 cms); black tip to tail.

Weasel: Less than 10″ (25 cms); no noticeable black tip to tail.

FUR ON WIRE

Where animal paths lead under barbed-wire fences, tufts of hair caught on the barbs can often be found and thus the user of the path can be identified. Look for tracks as well.

Roe deer hair is fairly coarse and brown or gingery

Badger hair is coarse and black with white tips

Fox hair is soft and usually gingery-brown or black

HAZEL NUT CLUES

Hazel can be found in the area covered by these walks, so it might be of interest to look out for any discarded hazel shells found near these trees. Small mammals have characteristic ways of opening the nuts and by examining the marks left on the shells the species of animal may be identified.

Dormouse

Showing the smooth inside surface to the hole with toothmarks around it on the shell surface.

Bank vole

Showing only corrugated toothmarks around the edge of the hole and no markings on the shell surface.

Woodmouse

Showing toothmarks similar to those of the bank vole – around the inside of the hole but with markings on the shell surface as well.

Squirrel

Splits nut into halves along the seam, sometimes nipping the top off first. Young squirrels make quite a mess of a hazel-nut shell when they are first learning the art.

SKULLS AND BONES

Surprisingly few skulls and bones are found in the countryside. Many dead creatures are eaten by scavengers, some of which, like the fox, also remove and hide this source of food. Others are buried by beetles or are covered with leaves or undergrowth. The diggings from badgers' setts are a good place to look as are discarded bottles and owl pellets. A hand-lens or magnifying glass may be needed to identify the smaller skulls. Skulls make interesting finds and can be readily identified using books on tracks and signs (see bibliography, page 124).

Rabbit skull

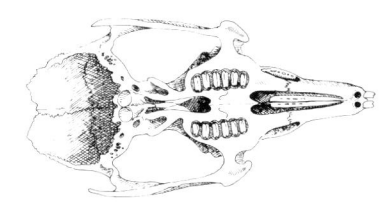

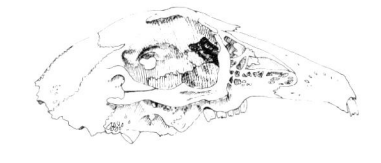

Underside of skull   *Side view skull, lower jaw missing*

ANIMAL TRACKS

The budding nature detective can learn a great deal from animal tracks. Snow is best especially when it is fairly shallow; tracks can be followed for miles if animals have been active during the night. Sand is also a good medium if arriving before the crowds. Firm mud is fine for recording tracks, either with plaster of Paris or wax – these will not work very well in sand and not at all in snow.

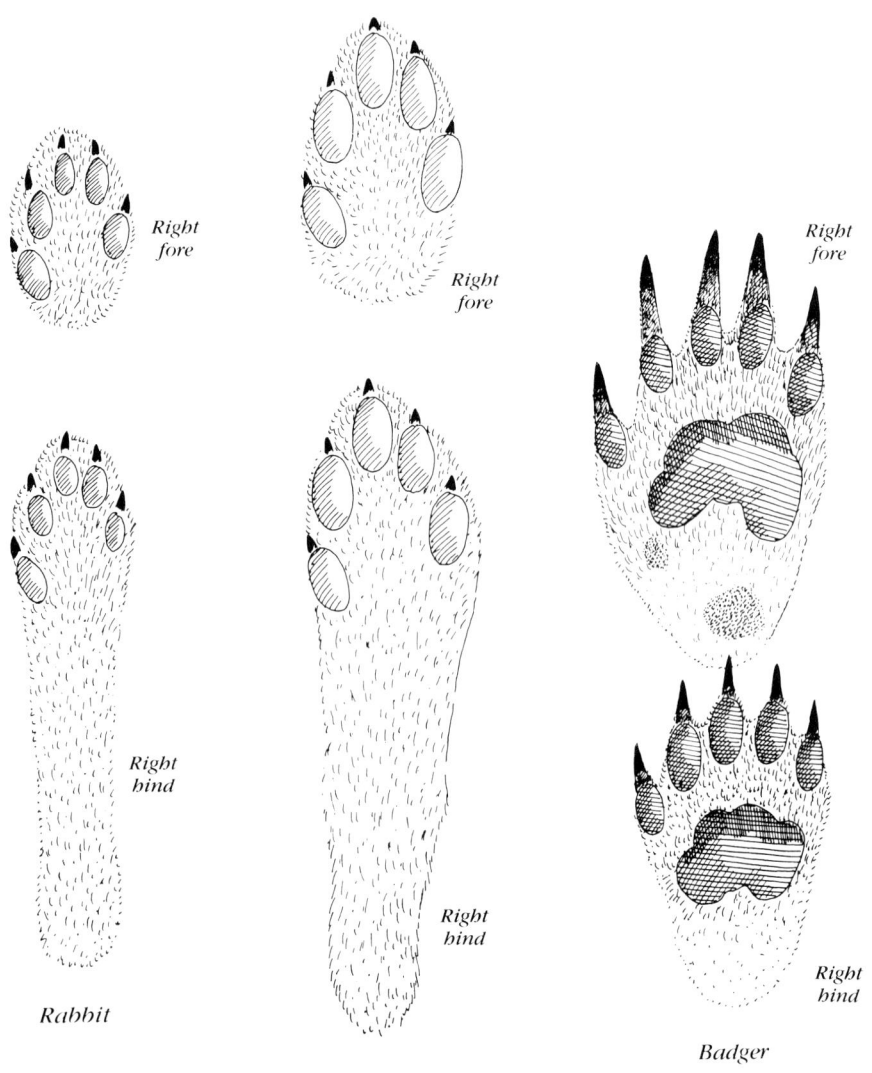

Rabbit — Right fore, Right hind

Hare — Right fore, Right hind

Badger — Right fore, Right hind

Squirrel

Mink

Hedgehog

Water vole

Stoat

Roe deer

Dog

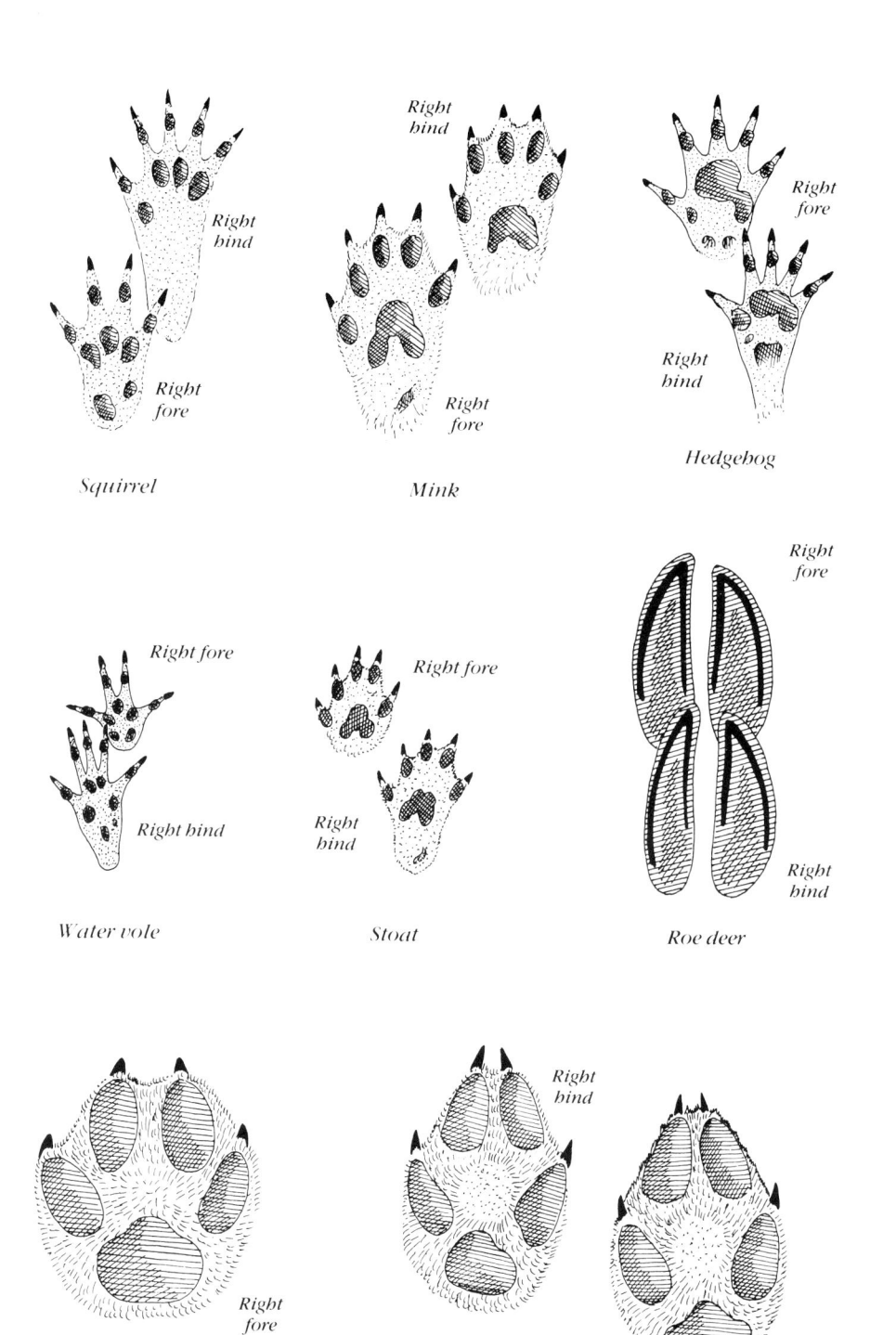

Fox

119

SEA SHELLS

Sea shells can be divided into a number of different types. There are those like land snails – the winkle and the whelk; limpets which fasten themselves flat to rocks and move around slowly to feed; and finally there are bivalves which consist of two matching halves. Mussels cling in groups with threads to rocks or pier legs while cockles and razor shells bury themselves at differing depths in sandy mud.

Common limpet

Common/edible cockle

Common winkle

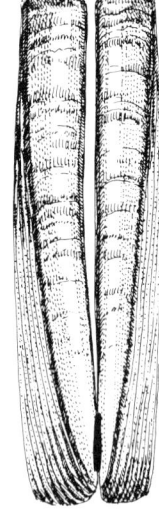

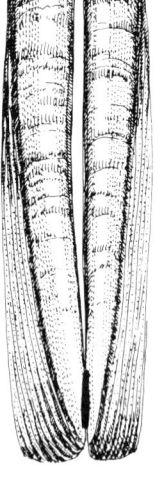

Razor shell

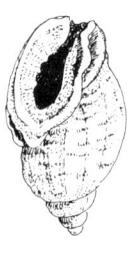

Dog whelk

Common whelk

Common mussel

INSECTS and SPIDERS

General rules:

Insects have:
 4 wings
 6 legs
 2 antennae
 three-part body

The insect class includes:
 beetles
 moths
 butterflies
 dragonflies and damsel flies
 ants and aphids
 bees and wasps
 flies

Bumble bee

Damsel fly

Dragonfly

Spiders have:
 no wings
 8 legs
 head and body

Spiders belong to a class called *arachnida*, which includes:
 harvestmen
 scorpions
 mites
 ticks

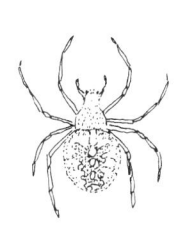

Common garden spider

WILDLIFE AND THE LAW

Under the 1981 Wildlife and Countryside Act, a large number of species gained special protection. Set out below are some guidelines to the Act.

Plants:
It is illegal to pick or to take any part of some 92 plants and included in this list are many orchids and the Cheddar pink. It is forbidden to dig up any wild plant unless the permission of the landowner has been obtained.

Reptiles and Amphibians:
It is illegal to catch, injure or kill:
    the Great Crested Newt   the Sand Lizard
    the Natterjack Toad   the Smooth Snake
It is forbidden to kill or injure or offer for sale:
    the Grass Snake   the Slow-worm
    the Viporous Lizard
It is an offence to offer for sale either alive or dead:
    the Adder   the Palmate Newt
    the Common Frog   the Smooth Newt
    the Common Toad
and it is forbidden to offer for sale any other native reptiles and amphibians.

Mammals:
Some mammals, like the bat, dormouse and the otter, are totally protected, therefore it is illegal to disturb them or even to damage their homes or prevent access to where they live. Other mammals, like the badger, have partial protection, which makes it illegal to kill or injure or to be in possession of a live or recently-killed badger.

Birds:
The law relating to birds is rather complex and if details are needed, the RSPB will help. Broadly speaking all wild birds, their eggs, and their occupied nests are protected by law from theft, disturbance, killing or taking. The exceptions are a few species which can be shot for sport or food, or are considered 'pests'.

If you cause no harm to wildlife and follow the Country Code, you should stay on the right side of the law!

LIST OF ORGANISATIONS

Somerset Trust for Nature Conservation
Fyne Court, Broomfield, Bridgwater, Somerset TA5 2EQ.

Avon Wildlife Trust
Old Police Station, 32 Jacobs Wells Road, Bristol BS8 1DR.

Royal Society for Nature Conservation
The Green, Nettleham, Lincolnshire LN2 2NR.

Royal Society for the Protection of Birds
The Lodge, Sandy, Bedfordshire SG19 2DL.

The British Trust for Ornithology
Beech Grove, Tring, Hertfordshire HP23 5NR.

The Mammal Society
Baltic Exchange Buildings, 21 Bury Street, London EC3A 5AU.

The National Trust
42 Queen Anne's Gate, London SW1H 9AS.

Try your library for a list of local natural history clubs and societies.

BIBLIOGRAPHY

The Natural History of Britain and Europe (W. H. Smith)

Collins Gem Guides to: *Wildflowers*   *Trees*
(Genuine pocket-   *Butterflies and Moths*   *Wild Animals*
sized guides)   *Birds*   *Mushrooms and Toadstools*

Collins Pocket Guide to: The Seashore – Barrett and Yonge

Collins Field Guide to: *The Trees of Britain and Northern Europe* – Mitchell
    The Birds of Britain and Europe –
      Peterson, Mountfort and Hollom
    The Mammals of Britain and Europe – Van Den Brink

Collins Guide to Animal Tracks and Signs – Bang and Dahlstrom

Collins: The Wild Flowers of Britain and Northern Europe –
  Fitter, Fitter and Blamey

Mammal Watching – Michael Clark (Nature Watch)

Pond Watching – Paul Sterry (Nature Watch)

Mammals of Britain: Their Tracks, Trails and Signs –
  Lawrence and Brown (Blandford)

Nature Detective – Hugh Falkus (Hienemann)

The Birdlife of Britain – Hayman and Burton (Mitchell Beazley/RSPB)

Trees in Britain, Europe and North America – Roger Phillips (Pan)

Wild Flowers of Britain – Roger Phillips (Pan)

Grasses, Ferns, Mosses and Lichens of Great Britain and Ireland –
  Roger Phillips (Pan)

INDEX

adder (viper) 67
alder 31,32,35
ambrosia beetle 46
Anchor Head 71
angelica 22,32,33
aphids 15
ash 16,41,44,45,51,52,61,62
Avon Wildlife Trust 21

badger 14,15,26,35,41,42,44,
  52,53,54,55,77,96,101
barnacle
  acorn Australian 76
  acorn British 76
  stalked (goose) 107
bat 51
  greater horseshoe 66
  noctule 51
  pipistrelle 91
Beacon Hill 63,65
beech 14,66
Berrow Church 102,104
bilberry *see whortleberry*
birch 31,33,35
Birnbeck Pier 71,78
bittersweet
  see nightshade, woody
black bryony 93
Black Mountains 64
blackthorn 21,61,93
blaeberry *see whortleberry*
Blagdon and Lake 64
Blue Anchor 76
bluebell 13
bracket fungi 15
bramble 53
Brean Down 66,71
Brecon Beacons 64
Bridgwater and Bridgwater
  Bay 66,78,94,104
Bristol 76
Bristol Waterworks
  Company 45,47
buckthorn, sea 103
bullhead 33
bulrush (greater reedmace)
  36,37
burdock 32,36
Burnham-on-Sea 94,98
Burrington Combe 62,63
Butcombe Mill 26
buttercup 26,52

butterfly
  common blue 25
  gatekeeper 57
  large cabbage white 62
  marbled white 62
  peacock 43,44
  red admiral 43,44
  small skipper 24
  small tortoiseshell 43
  speckled wood 21,57

Callow Quarry 66
caloplaca thallincola 73
campion
  bladder 73
  red 44
  sea 73
Cheddar and Gorge 25,45,62,
  66,71,92
cherry, wild 22
Chew River 44,45
Chewton Mendip 45
Chew Valley Lake 64
chickweed 35
chiff-chaff 46
cinnabar moth 104
Clevedon 78
cockle 108
Congresbury Yeo River 81,82
Coombe Lodge 21
coot 37,47
Corsican pine 21,66
cow parsley 31,32,44
Crook Peak 94
cross leaved heath 64
crow 31
cuckoo 43
curlew 38,105,106
cuttlefish 108

damsel fly 22,37
  red 37
dandelion 24,32,36
Defoe, Daniel 94
dog fish, lesser spotted 108
dog's mercury 13,25
dogwood 21,42,53
dormouse 13
dragonfly 34,37
  ruddy darter 37
  southern hawker 37
dung beetle 96
dunlin 105

dunnock (hedge-sparrow)
  81,82
Dutch elm disease 46,93

East Brent 98
East Twin Brook 66
East Twin Swallet
  (Swallow Hole) 66
Ebbor Gorge 62
eel 34
elder 51,52,76,77,78,93
elm 46,93,98
Exmoor 94

fern
  bracken 62,63,68
  hart's tongue 12
  maidenhair spleenwort 54
  polypody 17,44,52
  soft shield 12
fieldfare 42
field maple 21,42,53,56
fir 47
firecrest 81
Flat Holm 66,71,94
fox 22,31,35,41,44,82,84,101
frog, common 34,85,86,97

Gatekeeper 57
Getty, John Paul, junior 35
glasswort 71,72
Glastonbury Tor 57,94
goldcrest 16,81
goldfinch 36,83
goosander 37
gorse 63
grass
  lyme 103
  marram 103
  purple moor 63
  sea couch 103
  Timothy 24
  Yorkshire fog 24
grass snake 67,85,86
grebe, great crested 24
Grebe Swallet 67
groundsel 36

hare 38,102
hawkmoth 95
hawkmoth, privet 95
hawthorn 21,42,53,82,93

125

hazel 13,21,53
heather (ling) 63
  bell 64
  common 64
hedgehog 58,102
Hedgehog Protection Society 52
hedge mustard 62
hedge sparrow *see dunnock*
hemp agrimony 27
hen harrier 37
Henry VIII 78
hermit crab 75
heron 23,31,33,35,82,83
hog weed 32
holly 21,44,42
honeysuckle 95
horse chestnut 44,87
house martin 68

iris, yellow 31,37
ivy 12,54
ivy-leaved toadflax 54

jackdaw 25
jay 16

kestrel 35,84
kingfisher 33,34,35
knapweed 24,26

Land's End 76
larch 15,16,21,45,58,66
lark 31
lime 14,15,22
limpet 108
ling (cross-leaved heath) 64
Little River 84,85

magpie 86,97
mallard 23,48,77,78
Mammal Society 34
mayweed 24
meadow pipit 64
meadowsweet 31,33
Mill Inn 26
Minehead 76
minnow 34
mistletoe 15
moorhen 37,47
mussel 108

nail galls 15
National Trust 71,78,93,94,95
Nature Conservancy Council 35
newt, great crested 97
nightshade
  deadly 28
  enchanter's 25
  woody 28

North Hill 63,65

oak 11,13,17,18,22,24,45,46, 52,61,98
old man's beard (traveller's joy) 54,71
otter 34
owl 85
  little 41
  tawny 41
oyster catcher 105,106

Parrett River 94,104
Peak District National Park 62
peewit (lapwing) 28,31,38
Pen Hill 54,63,66
pigeon 31
pineapple weed 26
Polden Hills 66
poplar, white 78
Priddy 63
primrose 14
  evening 103
privet 92,93,97
purple loosestrife 22,23
pygmy shrew

Quantocks 66,94

rabbit 38,42,54,71,72,77,93, 101,102
ragwort 104
ramsons (wild garlic) 14
red valerian 43
redwing 42
reed 35,43,104
reedmace 35
rhododendron 16
ribwort plantain 26
robin 64
rock samphire 72
Rod's Pot 67
roe deer 18,35,53,54,56
rook 25,31
rowan (mountain ash) 68,76
Rowberrow Warren 25,66

St. Thomas Becket 78
Sand Bay
sanderling 105
scabious 52,53
Scots pine 15,16,35,66
scurvy grass 72,73
Severn Bridge 78
shelduck 106,107
Shepton Mallet 63
shoveler 23
shrew
  common 84
  pygmy 84

Sidcot School Speleological Society 67
Sidcot Swallet 67
skate (common ray) 107,108
skylark 64
sloe
snapdragon 54
soldier beetle 32
Somerset Trust for Nature Conservation 35,51,57
sooty-mould 15
spindle tree 45
spruce – sitka and Norway 21, 45,52,66
spurge, sea 104
squirrel, grey or red 14,55, 86,87
starling 41,51
Steep Holm 27,66,71,94
stickleback 33,34
stinging nettle 43,52
stonechat 64,65
Street 66
swallow 68
swan, mute 31,33,88
sycamore 14,16,98

tar spot 14
teasel 36
thistle 24,36,83
  creeping 22
thrift 72
thrush 42
Tickenham Hill 78
tits 15,21,51
  blue 15
  coal 15
  great 15
toad 102
tufted duck 48

Uphill 94

Velvet Bottom 67
verrucaria maura 73
viper *see adder*
vole 84
  bank 13,42,85
  field 82

wagtail
  grey 48
  pied 48
  yellow 48
warbler
  reed 35,43
  willow 46
wasp 14
Wells 63
Wemberham Villa 82

Wesley, John 94
Weston-super-Mare 27,66,78,
  82,94,102
Weston Woods 71
West Twin Brook 66
wheatear 64,65
whelk – common and dog 75,
  76,108
white beam 22
white deadnettle 44
whortleberry (bilberry/
  blaeberry) 63,64
wild rose 21

willow 31,35,97
willowherb 25
  hairy 23
  rosebay 22,43
winkle 75,108
witches' broom 33
wood anemone 14
woodmouse 13,14,42,84,85
woodpecker 41,51
  great spotted 17
  green 17,28
Woodspring Museum 82,94
Woodspring Priory 78

Wookey Hole 45
World Wildlife Fund 35
Worlebury Hill 27,71
wrack
  bladder 75
  egg 75
  flat 75
wren 81,82,84
Wrington 66

yellow poppy 52
yew 18,98

OTHER TITLES IN THE *WILDLIFE WALKABOUTS* SERIES

THE LIZARD to MID-CORNWALL
by Keith Spurgin
illustrated by Mo Tingey
£4.50
ISBN 0-948264-03-9   1987

LAND'S END PENINSULA
by Des Hannigan
illustrated by John Kempster
£4.50
ISBN 0-948264-01-2   1986

SOUTH COTSWOLDS and NORTH AVON
by Rosemary Teverson
illustrated by Julia Morland
£4.95
ISBN 0-948264-02-0   1986
(Reprinted 1989)

BIRMINGHAM and the BLACK COUNTRY
by Peter Shirley
illustrated by Julia Morland
£4.95
ISBN 0-948264-04-7   1988

Prices are correct at time of going to press.

All available from good bookshops especially in the areas they cover.

In case of difficulty please contact the publishers:
Wayside Books
3 Park Road, Clevedon, Avon BS21 7JG
Telephone (0272) 874750